C000091283

Light in our Lockdown

Gathering the scattered
Thoughts for the Day
of Ampthill Baptist Church

Edited by Andrew Goldsmith

Unless otherwise indicated, all Scripture quotations are taken from the Holy Bible, New International Version Anglicised Copyright © 1979, 1984, 2011 Biblica. Used by permission of Hodder & Stoughton Ltd, an Hachette UK company. All rights reserved. 'NIV' is a registered trademark of Biblica UK, trademark number 1448790.

Scripture quotations marked (NLT) are taken from the Holy Bible, New Living Translation, copyright © 1996, 2004, 2007, 2013, 2015 by Tyndale House Foundation. Used by permission of Tyndale House Publishers, Inc., Carol Stream, Illinois 60188. All rights reserved.

Scripture quotations marked (ESV) are from the ESV® Bible (The Holy Bible, English Standard Version®), copyright © 2001 by Crossway, a publishing ministry of Good News Publishers. Used by permission. All rights reserved.

Cover design by Steph Phillips.

All text and photos used with permission.

Copyright © 2020 Andrew Goldsmith

All rights reserved.

ISBN: 9798655592353

DEDICATION

The proceeds from this book will be shared between two Christian charities whom we support as a local church, both doing amazing work around the world: **Mission Aviation Fellowship** and **Open Doors**.

www.maf-uk.org

MAF's vision is to see 'isolated people physically and spiritually transformed in Christ's name.' They use aviation and technology, because in many places those are the only ways to reach isolated people in need.

www.opendoorsuk.org

Open Doors works in over 60 countries, supplying Bibles, training church leaders, providing practical support and emergency relief, and supporting Christians who suffer for their faith. Over 260 million Christians are persecuted for their faith worldwide. In the UK and Ireland Open Doors works to raise awareness of global persecution, mobilising prayer, support and action among Christians.

CONTENTS

ACKNOWLEDGMENTS

With sincere gratitude to all those who contributed and went beyond their comfort zone to write and share for others. Thanks to Lauren Herbert for beautiful artwork with the ABC online weekday reflections, to Steph Phillips for the cover design and sermon note illustration, and to the church family of Ampthill Baptist Church for your encouragement, love and prayers for one another, especially during the lockdown of 2020.

Therefore encourage one another and build each other up, just as in fact you are doing.

1 Thessalonians 5:11

FOR THE SON OF MAN CAME TO

seek & save

THE LOST.

Luke 19:10

INTRODUCTION

During the lockdown of 2020, 'coronatime', the church across the UK and beyond endured difficulties and sorrow along with the rest of society. It also saw a burst in creative energy, innovation and activity as it sought to continue to look up to God and trust ourselves into his care, to look outwards in serving and supporting local communities and the church family, and look inwards to deepen and grow in faith. The church buildings were closed but by faith in Christ, depending on the Holy Spirit, the church was alive and well. Pandemics can't shut down what God is doing.

As part of this, the scattered church of Ampthill Baptist Church were just one small part of God's global family, his kingdom people on earth, and we also sought to hold fast to the Lord, to care for and support our local neighbours and the vulnerable, and to encourage one another in faith – not least while we were unable to meet and encourage one another in person.

The church throughout history has grown when it has met around the word of God faithfully preached, as it has sung songs and brought its worship and prayers, and been humbled, fed and renewed around the communion meal shared. All this and more – the fun and fellowship, the hugs and physical touch of comfort or affirmation, the meals and groups and games and more across all ages ... stopped. Lockdown began in March 2020.

Scattered, but still belonging, we continued to be worshippers, disciples and missionaries. Apart for a time, not face to face, yet longing to be with one another, we were active in prayer, online and connecting in other ways.

This series of *Thought for the Day* was produced in that time, one simple way to offer a piece of daily bread, food for the day from God's word, to encourage us in our walk with God and our life in Christ together. Whilst apart it also enabled us to hear from one another, and share our stories. They were shared across the church and online during 2020. This book collects these together in testimony to God's faithful care and a reminder of the blessing of being one in Christ.

My hope is that these short reflections might continue to speak and sustain spiritual life, to connect us with God and his word, and build up disciples of Jesus. He is our light at all times, even and especially in dark places.

May God bless you, Andrew

*Your word is a lamp to my feet
and a light for my path.*

Psalm 119:105

Faith

by Andrew Goldsmith

Now faith is being sure of what we hope for and certain of what we do not see. **Hebrews 11:1**

Ampthill Baptist Church (the building) has a motto on the front beneath the sundial: "Carpe Diem" – seize the day. I'm not sure that the sundial works but the motto is certainly worth remembering. That sense of making the most of the opportunity of the day or the moment. Go for it. Be bold. It conjures up the sense of confidence, decisiveness or action. There is a time for such things, a time to act. For today that might be knocking on a neighbour's door to offer help, sending a card, stopping to pray, phoning someone. There's also a time to reflect, pause, consider, pray. Not every moment is a time to respond in action. God is never in a hurry.

What might an ancient church have had as its motto, carved over the doorway? As we read the New Testament, three words ring out across the varied congregations and clusters of believers: *faith, hope and love*.

Christian faith has an object: God and his promises, Christ and his achievements, the reality of new life with the Spirit as our guarantee. It is not a vague feeling, it is not being religious, it is rooted in our mind and heart and flows in action and priorities. These realities of God – Father, Son and Holy Spirit – do not change even when a pandemic appears, even when we don't know what happens next. These are a solid rock-like foundation for faith. Faith is not strong because we *feel* we have strong faith (often we don't), it is strong because our God is strong, and he holds his people.

So may we be sure of God, that he is good and he is with us. May we be sure of what he has said, and content that we don't need to know all the answers. And may faith bring his peace and assurance into us, spur us into action, and draw us to prayer. May faith arise.

Hope

by Shaggy Abdon Shortley

*May the **God of hope** fill you with all joy and peace as you trust in Him, so that you may **overflow with hope** by the power of the Holy Spirit.*
Romans 15:13

It's just occurred to me that we use the word "hope" an awful LOT! Here are just some of the ways I've used it in the last couple of days:

Hope you and your family stay virus-free. Hope my mum's cancer doesn't recur. Hope I'll find some eggs at Tesco today (I miss eggs!).

Our everyday expressions of hope are our desires for good things to happen. But there are no guarantees we'll find the items we need at any grocery. No guarantees we or any of our loved ones won't catch Covid-19 or get ill in some way. We could cross our fingers, touch wood and hope with all our heart --- our wishes may or may not be fulfilled.

Our Christian hope, however, is based on *the **God of hope** Himself!* When we remember what He has done for us in Jesus, what He is continuing to do in our lives today, and the promises He will fulfill when Jesus returns, we realise that our hope is not wishful thinking. It is confident expectation. It is grounded on God who is unchangeable, reliable, faithful and eternal.

As the song "Jesus, Hope of the Nations" goes:

> *You are the hope living in us,*
> *You are the rock in whom we trust,*
> *You are the light shining for all the world to see;*
> *You rose from the dead conquering fear,*
> *Our Prince of Peace drawing us near,*
> *Jesus our hope, living for all who will receive -*
> *Lord, we believe!*

During this strange and unsettling time of being locked down, let's motivate one another to **trust in Him.** Why? Because when we trust in God, He fills us **with all joy and peace** whatever the situation.

Are you struggling to trust and have hope today? Let's ask the **Holy Spirit** to help us **overflow with hope**.

Love

by Diane Maple

Do read the whole of 1 Corinthians chapter 13 as it has lots to say about **love**. The final verse says:

*And now these three remain, faith, hope and love. But the greatest of these is **love**.* **1 Corinthians 13:13**

Love is patient

We have been told that there have been queues at most supermarkets and some people have waited for almost an hour to gain access to a shop often to get items for other people who are not able to go out. Most of the queues shown on television have been very orderly with people keeping a 2 metre distance between them – love and patience in action!

Love is kind

In these unprecedented times communities are coming together to support vulnerable people in their neighbourhood. ABC has a list of volunteers who are shopping for those who are isolated at home. These volunteers are demonstrating God's love in a practical way. Our young neighbours have shown great kindness to us, 'the old couple in the corner'(!), offering to shop for us – our age and medical issues put us in the vulnerable group.

Love never fails

If you were watching *Songs of Praise* on Sunday you will remember Aled Jones' interview with a D-Day veteran. Now 93, and a committed Christian, he said 'Love is the strongest thing' and he referred to 1 Corinthians 13. He knew God's word. He had committed it to memory and he acknowledged that God's love had carried him through the devastation of war. God's love will carry us through the present situation.

The love of God is unique. The Bible tells us (Romans 5:8) that even when we did not love Him, God still loved us and loved us so much that He sent his only son to die on the cross to take away our sins - to be our Saviour. God loves us unconditionally. How do we love others? Andrew asked in his verse for the day on Monday 'What might the Lord ask of us at this time?' Our answer surely should be to show God's love in all we say and do. Love is one of the fruits of the Spirit. Jesus said, 'A new command I give you. Love one another as I have loved you' (John 13:34).

John and I are celebrating our golden wedding anniversary this coming weekend. We had planned celebrations with family and friends but that is not going to happen. As we look back on the past 50 years there have been many bumps along the road but we can testify to God's love for us through the good times and the bad.

As we all negotiate the coming weeks of uncertainty may we know and experience God's great love in our lives: his unfailing, unique, unconditional, sacrificial, personal love.

Jesus, the coming King

by Naomi Sherwood

After John was put in prison, Jesus went into Galilee, proclaiming the good news of God. 'The time has come,' he said. 'The kingdom of God has come near. Repent and believe the good news!' **Mark 1:14-15**

I wonder what kind of world Coronavirus has got you hoping for. Is it a world with less hoarding and more charity? Or perhaps, less poverty and more provision? Less isolation and more community?

At the opening of Mark's Gospel, the world is far from how it should be. The ruling leaders of the time are unjust, and society is strictly divided. In the middle of it all, religious persecution is high, with John the Baptist chained up for preaching about a coming king, the Messiah. God's people have been waiting for hundreds of years to see prophecies fulfilled. It's a world longing for some good news!

As he begins his teaching, Jesus' message is clear: 'The kingdom of God has come near. Repent and believe the good news.' It's news so good that Simon, Andrew, James and John immediately leave everything behind to follow Jesus, before they've even fully understood his meaning. With our perspective, with scripture fulfilled, we know why Jesus' message is so compelling.

The good news for a suffering world is that there is another kingdom. It's not injustice on the throne, but Jesus. It's not a kingdom that will perish, but a king who reigns eternally glorified. Yet how can Jesus say it has come near? How can we believe this is true in the midst of our world today?

Because Jesus himself has come near. He came into this world so that we might, through him, have access to the Father. The Son's suffering offers an end to ours. Jesus' two commands give a further glimpse of this coming kingdom: repent and believe. Trust in Jesus for complete salvation. As you do, turn from sin and leave it entirely behind.

What is the kingdom that Jesus has brought near? It's not a world of 'less' or 'more'. It is no sin, no death and no division. It is the complete fullness of sanctification, life, and adoption. What good news for our present sense of longing!

The Way of the Cross

by David Mead

The earthly journey of Jesus to the cross started with his birth at Bethlehem and ended on the cross at Calvary just outside Jerusalem. A journey of learning, leading, teaching, caring, healing and ultimately of sacrifice on the cross for the sake of believers throughout time. This was the fulfilment of the Old Testament prophesies and the purposes of God.

Holy week starts with the triumphal entry into Jerusalem, riding on a donkey, surrounded by people waving palms and, no doubt, shouting. A greeting by the people worthy of the king that he is. The people were looking for a saviour who would deliver them from the oppression of Roman occupation and the Pharisees, and they were expecting him to lead a revolution but this was not why he had come and by the end of the week they had turned against him.

Jesus continued teaching, healing and caring for his disciples and all who came to him seeking help. The meaning of much of his teaching was not understood until after the resurrection when the disciples thought back on his words. Then they understood that he had predicted what would happen and that he died and rose again for them and for all believers who should follow down through the ages including us today.

Yes, Jesus prayed for us at that last supper and he cares for us as he did for his disciples of old. Look back at your life, see the things he has done for you and the ways he has led you. These will not always be the ways you expected but they are His way for you.

Give thanks and remember that he will be with you and keep you who believe until the end of days.

Cast all your anxiety on him because he cares for you.
1 Peter 5:7

Prayer

By Marjorie Austin

This Maundy Thursday, the day of the Last Supper, we reflect on another meal:

The Israelites did as they were told; some gathered much, some little. And when they measured it by the omer, the one who gathered much did not have too much, and the one who gathered little did not have too little. Everyone had gathered just as much as they needed. **Exodus 16:17, 18**

Manna was given to the Israelites in their time of need, although they got a bit fed up with it after a bit! Manna translates 'what is it?' because it was a mystery, arriving day by day and keeping them fed, alive and able to follow God's plan for them.

This current enforced physical isolation is for our good, to keep us alive, and able to serve God and our community. And we can be forgiven if we get a bit fed up with it sometimes. Thank God for technology of various sorts, and for many of us, the time to be able to send messages of encouragement, wrap people around with 'virtual' comfort, and to pray for them.

Prayer is something we turn to, especially in our time of need, such as we are going through now, and prayer too is a mystery. We know from scripture that we should *pray continually, give thanks in all circumstances'* (1 Thess. 5:16) but we know too that *our Heavenly Father knows* our needs before we ask (Matt. 6:32).

Sometimes my prayer seems to be just me thinking in my head; occasionally I feel as though my heart is completely engaged with my prayers. Often I feel my prayer is wholly inadequate and I am very easily distracted!

So here is my encouragement: No-one had too much Manna, and no-one had too little of this mysterious 'what is it?' Manna. But they did need to gather it every day. And so with our prayer; we need every day to connect with our Heavenly Father, but we cannot pray too much, and He will sustain us with very little. What a wonderful God!

I hope you are encouraged too.

The Cross

by Andrew Goldsmith

And when the centurion, who stood there in front of Jesus, heard his cry and saw how he died, he said, "Surely this man was the Son of God!" **Mark 15:39**

On Good Friday we remember the events of the day that Jesus died. The last hours of his earthly life are full of darkness around him – the plots of those who were envious or despised Jesus, the betrayal by Judas for nothing but a bag of coins, his friends sleeping rather than praying with him and then abandoning him in his great hour of need, Peter blatantly lying to distance himself from Jesus. It leads to Jesus being increasingly isolated, facing threats and violence, and evil itself.

This distressing experience continues through a false trial and beatings, facing an angry mob, to a travesty of justice with a judge who washes his hands and then releases a murdered instead. Barabbas goes free, Jesus is condemned; the guilty one will be released, Jesus will die in his place. Jesus in righteous One is led out to die for us all.

Jesus is crucified. The Roman soldiers do their job. The Son of God, the Lord of glory, the glorious Beloved One of the Father goes to a place of humiliation, bearing shame, carrying our sin, receiving evil's worst, under the wrath of God on sins that were not his own. Alone, he bears this, he endures, he cries out, he finishes it. Then, only then, he dies.

As he hangs on that cross, even the skies grew dark in the middle of the day. Darkness without, darkness within, it seems darkness reigns. But this is only what could be seen. For he is the Light of the World and even though he dies he is unconquerable. The cross is not the end. Death will not have the last word, for him or – by a true and living faith joined to him – for us.

One man stands at the foot of the cross. A Roman centurion sees the bloodied victim. But he heard what Jesus said and he sees more: the Son of God.

Today may we see something afresh of what he did for us, even for you and me. And may we see how good, glorious, loving and powerful he is, this Jesus Christ, the Son of God.

Resurrection Hope

by Frank Sherburn

Take a few moments to read **John 20:10-29**

In **verse 16** Jesus said to her, "Mary."

> She turned toward him and cried out in Aramaic, "Rabboni!" (which means Teacher).

> Thomas said to him, "My Lord and my God!"

> Then Jesus told him, "Because you have seen me, you have believed; blessed are those who have not seen and yet have believed."

Easter Sunday, year Zero. What a day that was! Jesus who was dead and buried is alive! From that day the world would never be the same. No wonder people of the time were confused and many still are.

Our Bible reading focuses on two of Jesus's friends, Mary Magdalene and Thomas. Both of them had their lives turned upside down, having suffered grief at the loss of the one who had changed their lives, and then suddenly experiencing extreme joy and renewed faith through encountering the risen Jesus.

17

They had different reasons for not being able to realise the truth of the resurrection at first.

For Mary, her love and emotion clouded her vision; for Thomas it was his passion for the truth and his questioning heart that caused him to hesitate. Nevertheless, both, in the end, embraced the whole truth that Jesus was alive.

Mary is able to call Jesus, *'Rabboni'* – 'Teacher'. Thomas calls Jesus, 'My Lord and my God'.

What words do you use to the risen Jesus?

Here's what Jesus had to say about those who embrace Him:

> *'My sheep listen to my voice; I know them, and they follow me. I give them eternal life, and they shall never perish; no one can snatch them out of my hand.'* **John 10:27, 28**

This is the great Resurrection Hope that emerges from the empty tomb. A Hope not just for year Zero but for today also with all its uncertainties and for eternity.

Delighting in God's Good Words

by Mel Herbert

I am reading through the Bible in a Year, not with HTB but Selwyn Hughes, so I'm not quite in sync with the rest of you. However, I have been astonished on a number of days at how the 4 passages, Old Testament, Psalms, Proverbs and New Testament are in sync with each other. As I wrote this, (Saturday 4th April) the common theme was especially good.

The Israelites are on the verge of entering the promised land (**Deuteronomy 5:1 – 6:25**). Moses is giving them his last words and reminding them just how great the blessing of God will be *IF* they continue in His ways and follow His commands. They (and therefore we also) were reminded to "repeat them to your children. Talk about them when you sit in your house and when you walk along the road, when you lie down and when you get up. Bind them as a sign on your hand and let them be a symbol on your forehead. Write them on the doorposts of your house and on your gates." Let's learn to chat the goodness of God whenever the opportunity arises with those who believe and those who don't.

Then, David, in **Psalm 40:6-10** proclaims about himself that he "delights to do Your will, my God; Your instruction resides within me." Meditating on God's commands is going to make those instructions "reside" within us, then what comes out of our mouths will be glorifying to His name.

Proverbs 10:11 reminded me that, "The mouth of the righteous is a fountain of life ..." We can speak into all sorts of situations when we are filled with God's Spirit and we need to have confidence that God's way is the best way.

And then I came to **Luke 6:12-36** where Jesus, having chosen his 12 disciples, reminds us in the Beatitudes that if we consider ourselves to be spiritually poor, the Kingdom of heaven is ours; that if we are hungry for the things of God, He will fill us up, that those who weep now will laugh in the future and that if we are persecuted because we love Jesus, that our reward in Heaven will be great. He also adds, to those who will listen, a bunch of very practical commands about how we can love both our neighbours and our enemies, which circles right round to us keeping God's commands, knowing that He will bless us and those around us through what we say and do in obedience to Him.

We have that opportunity right now – in small ways and large. Let us love large and serve our God any way we can. He will bless what we do when we serve in obedience to His commands to love the Lord our God with all our hearts, all our strength and all our minds and love our neighbours as ourselves.

Forgiveness: a new start

by John Feil

"I get so excited Lord every time I realise, I'm a gibbon"

We sang this song in our Sunday night youth Bible study back in the early 80's (sometimes with monkey movements) and watched the reaction of our youth leaders (who later became my parents-in-law!). It's a great song — next time we are all together in church and I'm at the front with my guitar ...

But those were not the actual words. The excitement isn't "I'm a gibbon", but "I'm forgiven."

The realisation that we are forgiven and made right with God through the death and resurrection of Jesus is the key to our amazing journey of love with our heavenly Father and a very good reason to get so excited.

Psalm 103:10-12 says:

> *He does not treat us as our sins deserve*
> *or repay us according to our iniquities.*
> *For as high as the heavens are above the earth,*
> *so great is his love for those who fear him;*

as far as the east is from the west,
   so far has he removed our transgressions from us.

We have been let off without charge, justice has been served through the cross of Jesus, mercy triumphs. It's a love revolution that invites us to join in: to forgive others, to confess our sins, to leave the past behind, to become the humans God made us to be and to obey Jesus' command to love our neighbor.

Our excited celebration on earth when we realise we are forgiven is a reflection of the "rejoicing in the presence of the angels of God over one sinner who repents" (Luke 15:10).

The song continues and celebrates our past dealt with, grace in today, hope for what lies ahead.

We are forgiven: it's a new start, the slate is clean, we are free to love and forgive others ...

"Hallelujah, Lord, my heart just fills with praise."

Waiting on God

by Judith Coen

The LORD is good to those whose hope is in him, to the one who seeks him; it is good to wait quietly for the salvation of the LORD.
Lamentations 3:25-26

I'm not very good at waiting. If I have a jigsaw, I have to do it regardless of anything else that must be done. If I have a book, I have to read it into the night. If I have chocolate, I have to eat it – even if it is before dinner (or breakfast). I guess that all has to do with a lack of self-control as much as an inability to wait. Even so, waiting is hard. It goes against the nature of the culture we live in today. If we want something, we can have it straight away with the help of our credit cards. We can binge watch whole series of our favourite television programmes and we are forever trying to fill our time with 'useful' activities and new experiences.

But is this the way we should be living? When we look at our amazing natural world designed and created by God himself we see that, for at least three months of the year, it is lying dormant, resting and waiting, waiting for the word of the creator to bring it back to life again. However, this is not an unproductive time because while it waits, the world is being refreshed and prepared for the work that lies ahead.

We all have times of waiting in our lives. Now is a very obvious time, but we must all be able to think of times when we have been uncertain of a path we should take or a decision we should make, and we ask God for guidance and then we wait ... and we wait ... We seek him and we hope in him, and we wait. During that time, God is not ignoring us, but he is refining us and preparing us, giving us a time of rest and renewal, or maybe just allowing the suspense to build so that when our prayer is answered we are filled with an overflowing joy that is all the greater for the wait.

Let's not feel guilty about waiting quietly for the Lord; it requires peace, patience, faithfulness and self-control. Perhaps God is giving us time for these precious fruits to grow before he pours out his incredible goodness on us.

Peace, be still!

By Ruth Dant

And He (Jesus) arose and rebuked the wind and said unto the sea, "<u>Peace, be still</u>". And the wind ceased and there was a great calm. Jesus than went on to ask them, "Why is it that you are so fearful? How is it that you have no faith?"
Mark 4:39-40 (KJV)

Jesus had been preaching, teaching, casting out demons and healing all those who crowded around him asking him to do so all day and he was feeling, from a human point of view, utterly exhausted. So it is no surprise that he fell asleep almost as soon as his head touched the pillow, leaving his disciples to take him safely in their boat across the lake. Most of them were hardened fishermen, fishing had been their trade before he called them to become 'Fishers of men', so he completely trusted them.

Suddenly, as quite often happens on the Sea of Galilee I understand, a fierce storm arose. They had been in storms before but none like this one, the wind blew fiercely and the waves were so high that they came over into the boat. They were very frightened. Thinking they would drown they woke up Jesus, probably expecting him to come and help them bail out the boat, but instead, immediately seeing the situation he rebuked the winds and the waves and there was a great calm, or as we might say, "the sea became like a millpond" so that they were able to continue their journey to the other shore.

As they did so they looked at each other and said, "What manner of man is this that even the winds and the sea obey him?" At that moment they thought of him as 'just a man', not realising that he had complete authority over the winds and the waves; the elements had to obey him when he commanded them to be still. He had already chided them for their lack of faith and this was presumably because they had seen him do many miracles of healing, but hadn't realised he had power over the elements too.

Many people think of this account as being there to show us that God can calm the storms that arrive in our lives. Of course he can and does calm the storms we often face, but I believe that the account is there to show his power over nature as well as over humanity, that he was indeed a miracle worker because he was, in fact, the Son of God.

But what has this to do with the coronavirus, you may say. If, like me, you are quite used to being alone, then having to isolate oneself because you are told you are a vulnerable person is not really difficult. I have found the Lord has given me a much greater peace than I have ever experienced before and if I feel lonely then I can always talk to Him. Obviously I miss being taken to things like Fellowship Lunch and Fellowship Praise, etc., and of course I am not insensitive to those in the Fellowship who have asked for prayer for their loved ones and friends who have been affected in any way, and the need also to comfort those who have lost loved ones, either by card, letter or through the media. I am appalled too at the terrible loss of life over the whole country, but we can, like the disciples, ask Jesus to calm the wind and the waves of this virus knowing that we can leave everything in His hands. We can also ask him to fill us with his peace, which as the following verse says, passes all understanding.

I pray that *"the peace of God which passes all understanding, shall keep your hearts and minds through Christ Jesus."* **Philippians 4:7**

AND HE AROSE
AND REBUKED THE WIND
AND SAID UNTO THE SEA

PEACE,
BE STILL.

AND THE WIND CEASED
AND THERE WAS A GREAT CALM

Mark 4:39 KJV

God is with us

by Pete Davies

"Have I not commanded you? Be strong and courageous. Do not be afraid; do not be discouraged, for the Lord your God will be with you wherever you go." **Joshua 1:9**

Many of you may not know I grew up in a non-Christian household. We only attended a carol concert, wedding, christening or funeral. The closest I really came to Christianity was every now and then a very, very old vicar would come to my middle school and bore us for half an hour, that and my mum telling me I should read the Bible: 'it will teach you a lot'. I never did! Regardless of this lack of Christian input, I have never doubted that God was real, I just didn't do anything about it.

My family, like so many, have had our fair share of life thrown at us, some very significant and extremely stressful events, many just the normal day—to-day challenges. For instance, I was rushed to hospital on our honeymoon (*I was only testing the "in sickness and in health" clause!*). Sheryl developed a progressive disorder 2 years after we were married (*she was testing the clause!*). Nyah was born 2 months early (*she's just trouble*). We had car crashes in 2007 and 2014 and many of you do know that in recent years Sheryl has suffered with an exceptionally rare medical disorder, **twice:** *once whilst we were 850 miles away in Austria and* the other which left her with permanent scarring and relentless pain in her foot.

However, throughout all the above and much more, I was sure God was there. Don't get me wrong, there were plenty of times in the early hours of the morning looking at our tiny daughter in neonatal care, or driving 18 hours straight to get to a hospital, or seeing your wife connected to a plethora of machines when I thought *"Come on God, what are you playing at? Enough is enough"*, but looking back objectively, He was there! Nyah and Sheryl both had Christian NHS staff looking after them in the maternity and neonatal wards. On honeymoon, we prayed for an English-speaking person and one arrived literally a minute later. Travelling 18 hours home across 5 countries we made it onto the last Eurotunnel crossing, and twice when Sheryl's life has been literally in the balance, God has reassured us through His Church and the love and prayers of our extended Christian family.

The most notable confirmation I have had that He is with us was following our car accident at the once infamous Millbrook Crossing. Our car was on its side. Ambulances, fire engines, police were all in attendance. Sheryl had to be cut out of the car and Nyah had been removed and given to a couple who had stopped to help. Throughout the entire incident there was one man who seemed to be everywhere: liaising with the emergency services, the people caring for Nyah, my parents and us. Once things were in control, he came up to me, took my hand and said to me "God is with you, and he will always be with you!" Then he left.... Those words have been with me ever since. During all the subsequent illnesses, the accidents, the hospital admissions, the desperately worrying and lonely times watching Sheryl fight for life, I have always recalled that moment and those words, 'God is with you and He will always be with you!'

The reason I chose Joshua 1:9 out of the hundreds of verses in the Bible which refer to God being with us, or not forsaking us, or "He is with you", (*and there are hundreds, I checked with Andrew*) is the last seven words. **'God will be with you wherever you go'.** He is with you now, during these challenging and strange times. He is with you when you are at your lowest, when you feel vulnerable, when you are lonely, when you feel isolated. He is with you when you are desperate and, lest we forget, He is also with you during the happy and joyful times.

We may have to adhere to social distancing at the moment but at the same time, keep your distance from doubt, isolate yourself from fear and trust in God through it all, **for the Lord your God will be with you wherever you go!**

FOR THE WAGES OF SIN IS DEATH, BUT THE *gift of God is eternal life* IN CHRIST JESUS, OUR LORD.

Romans 6:23

God's gift of new life

By Jo Reynolds

For the wages of sin is death, but the gift of God is eternal life in Christ Jesus our Lord.   **Romans 6:23**

Life in Lockdown is real.

It seems as if, in recent weeks, science fiction has become reality, as we are living a new and different life which we could never have foreseen a few months ago.

Acts of selflessness by NHS and care workers, risking their own lives to save others, are being reported in the news every day. There are people giving care to someone they love, to shield them from Covid19, with little support and no respite.

The gifts are given freely and willingly, out of love for the recipient.

Eternal Life is real

Once, when I was walking locally, taking photos of Spring, I noticed fresh green bracken shoots growing through old, dead vegetation, an awakening. Later, I realized it was a picture with spiritual meaning, this new life was shaped like an opening heart, reminding me of the reality of new life in Christ.

The Bible says in 1 John 5:11, *'And this is the testimony: God has given us eternal life, and this life is in His Son.'*

When we receive Christ as our Saviour, our hearts are softened by the power of the Holy Spirit and are no longer focused on sin but turned towards God. We have been given new life and are adopted into God's family (Ephesians 1:5). This new spiritual life, created by God our Heavenly Father is new in nature. Our desire is to become more like Jesus, and we are no longer slaves to sin, although we still wrestle with it.

After the shepherds visited the new-born Saviour Jesus and spread the word about what the angels had told them, all who heard were amazed. But *'Mary treasured up all these things and pondered them in her heart'* (Luke 2:19). Like Mary, may we reflect on the good things God has given us to sustain our lives now and the hope we have in Him for eternity.

The Good Shepherd

by Martha Spencer

I am the good shepherd. I know my own and my own know me, just as the Father knows me and I know the Father; and I lay down my life for the sheep.
John 10:14-15

Normally, when I think of a shepherd, I think of someone dressed up in a tea towel and bedsheet enacting the nativity or a parable of Jesus. But, in reality, being a shepherd is a really hard job! As a shepherd it is your job to protect your dependent and defenceless flock – to lead them, care for them and keep them safe. So when Jesus calls himself the Good Shepherd, he is saying that he is our protector and companion. In Psalm 23, David speaks of God as his Shepherd who gives us rest, restores his soul and leads us all the way through the shadow of death into the house of the Lord. Our Good Shepherd is our eternal protector and guide.

But not only this, Jesus knows us as his own. It is such a privilege to be known personally, intimately and lovingly by our Lord Jesus Christ. 2 Timothy 2:19 says,

But God's firm foundation stands, bearing this seal: The Lord knows those who are his.

What a comfort this is for this overwhelming and isolating time – for those of us who follow Christ, we can trust that we belong to God as part of his family. As we have seen, he will not leave our side. What is more is that we also know Jesus – perhaps we can view this lockdown period as a time to get to know him better through scripture and prayer. Being known and knowing Jesus means we have fellowship with him forever. Our Good Shepherd is our eternal friend.

Finally, Jesus is the Good Shepherd who lays down his life for his sheep. There is no greater act of love than this (see John 15:13). Jesus sacrifices himself so that we might be spared from the wrath of God – we, the defenceless flock, need a rescuer and we have one in Jesus Christ. Jesus is not just a good shepherd – he's clearly got the skills of one – but he is THE Good Shepherd. He is the only one we need to guide us through this valley of the shadow of death, to bring us comfort, and to give us life eternal through his sacrifice.

Praise God that our Good Shepherd is our eternal guide, protector, friend and saviour! How precious it is to know him.

Shine like stars

By Tracey Feil

There was a season when Sarah was studying astronomy at Alameda and John embraced her interest and acquired a telescope so we could all gaze at the stars and planets up above in the dark, clear skies (obviously not that often, then!). We learnt together how to identify some of the constellations, clusters and individual stars in this hemisphere: Cassiopeia, Polaris, Orion for example. Who is not dazzled by the infinite array of patterns of light that twinkle down at us? It is good and right that we marvel at the stars and this leads us to declare the glory of the Lord, the creator of the heavens.

But we are called to do **more than** praise God for the stars he created. In Paul's letter to Philippi, he tells the followers of Christ to:

Shine among them like stars in the sky as you hold firmly to the word of life. **Philippians 2:15-16**

We are called to shine like stars in dark places; to shine like the brightness of the heavens.

I don't often feel very shiny.

So what does the word of life teach me about how to fulfil this command – to shine like stars?

Firstly, let's remember that ALL light comes from God. He is the source of light. It is He who says, 'let there be light.'

To shine we must experience His light in our lives. It is not my own light but His that will shine through me. A bit of science (not very accurate!) might help here: stars shine bright because they change hydrogen into helium in a process called nuclear fusion. That fusion creates their sparkle. What if we saw the power of the Holy Spirit within us as the act of nuclear fusion? We shine because of the Spirit fully at work within us. But where might the dark corners be, the parts of my life I don't let the Spirit into, that might dim my sparkle?

There are some **do**s and **don't**s in the passage too. We are told that we will shine when we:

- **do not** grumble or argue – hmmm, maybe tricky depending on who we are locked down with at the moment! But a good godly reminder to live without grumbling about our condition – remember Paul is writing this from his own locked-up cell and had a lot to grumble about but chose not to. (That doesn't mean we won't find it hard or struggle at times though.)

- **do** live clean lives, obedient to, or rooted in, His word.

Finally, sailors of old would use celestial navigation to find their way home. When we shine like stars, the purpose is to direct those lost in the dark to the Father, the source of all love and light and truth. As the people of Christ sparkle, may that be an encouragement to others and point them home to the greatness of God, sovereign over all.

It is an awesome mission. But, in the power of the Spirit, and by obedience to the word, let's dust ourselves off and shine for Him in these dark days, even if we don't feel very shiny ourselves.

And why not take an opportunity to go out onto our front step/back garden on a clear warm night, view the stars and sing with them about the greatness of our creator God?

(see also www.skymaps.com)

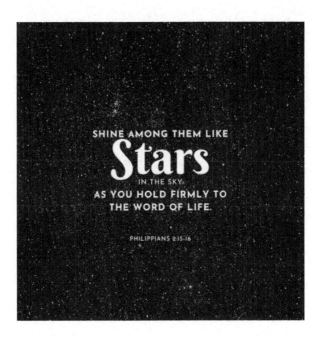

Salt of the earth

By Rob Baker

"You are the salt of the earth. But if the salt loses its saltiness, how can it be made salty again? It is no longer good for anything, except to be thrown out and trampled by men." **Matthew 5:13**

A few years ago, our family stayed the night beside the Saloum Delta in central Senegal (photo above). The land here is so low-lying and flat that sea water flows in, then dries out to leave salt deposits on the vast plains. This was once Africa's largest source of salt, producing over half a million tonnes per year (still over 200,000 today). The salt here needs three elements to be produced and gathered: **water**, **sunlight** and **the right environment**.

This got me thinking about our Christian life and witness.

WATER

Our new life in Christ needs to be flooding out to those around us; life in all abundance (John 10:10) which only He can give. As salt flavours and preserves, so water purifies and cleanses, and only Jesus can provide this. He says:

"Whoever drinks the water I give them will never thirst. Indeed, the water I give them will become in them a spring of water welling up to eternal life." (John 4:14)

LIGHT

The salt on the Saloum Delta is always there, but is inaccessible without the power of the sunlight. Similarly, a salt pot can sit proudly on our dining table, full to the brim. But if it is never picked up and shaken, it may as well not be there. If we are the salt of the earth, we need to use the salt, spread the salt, share the salt. In the same way that the sunlight draws out the salt, we should allow the light of Christ and His Holy Spirit to bring out His preserving, enriching goodness.

RIGHT ENVIRONMENT

1 Peter 3:15 tells us to always be ready to give a reason for the hope within us. Salt could not be produced in Senegal without the existence of a flat tidal estuary spanning many miles. We too need the right environment in which to share Christ, in a context which will genuinely speak to the lost, as Christ did through parables.

During these difficult times of confinement, we may wonder how we can share our faith. Yet research has shown an increase in those attending online services. There's always a way to share our faith, and we need to fervently pray for those opportunities. Because when we do, they happen.

The Holy Spirit who transforms us

by Lauren Herbert

Somehow the situation we're in lends itself quite well to thinking about "transformation."

With the announcement of a global pandemic our world as we knew it was transformed into a hand-washing, glove-wearing, toilet paper buying society, all for just a week or so before the announcement of lockdown really transformed our hustling, bustling way of life to empty roads and birdsong.

And during lockdown I feel like I have seen lots of transformations going on – parents transformed into teachers, bodies transformed by doing PE with Joe, rare ingredients like flour transformed into delicious bakes, and it all seems very exciting. But if you're anything like me, seeing all these apparent transformations on social media can easily lead to falling into the comparison trap.

The temptation is to respond by saying, "Praise God, our identity is in Christ and we don't need to undergo worldly versions of transformation to know that we are loved unconditionally by our Maker." And that is totally true. But it can so easily lead to us becoming complacent, and not stewarding our time well. Don't get me wrong, lockdown is tough for so many different reasons, and those reasons are different for each of us. We do absolutely need to be realistic with our time and energy, but lockdown has forced transformation on society as we knew it, so, shouldn't we, as the church, also be transforming during this time?

The mind-blowing fact is that whereas the transformation brought about by lockdown was forced upon us, the Holy Spirit who transforms us is given to us freely as a gift.

> *And the Spirit God gave us does not make us timid,*
> *but gives us power, love and self-discipline.*
> **2 Timothy 1:7**

The Holy Spirit transforms our minds, bringing a change of perspective and birthing creativity. He transforms our hearts, enabling us to love more and in ways we never thought we could. And these powerful transformations spur us into action, helping us to walk more in step with Jesus, becoming the people he created us to be.

And the first step to receiving the gift of the Holy Spirit is simply having the self-discipline to open it. Practice hearing His voice, even if you just spend 2 minutes each morning intentionally in His presence. Because the more you listen and look out for His voice, the more you will recognise how He speaks to you, and the more confident you will be that what you heard was Him.

After lockdown the world will probably not look quite the same as it did before, and neither should we. Because when all this is over, and it's already starting to happen, people will be looking for truth, hope and love. And we, as the body of Christ, not in our own strength but transformed by the Holy Spirit, will be ready.

Don't let lockdown pass you by, instead press into what God has for you – *a spirit not of timidity, but of power, love and self-discipline* (2 Timothy 1:7).

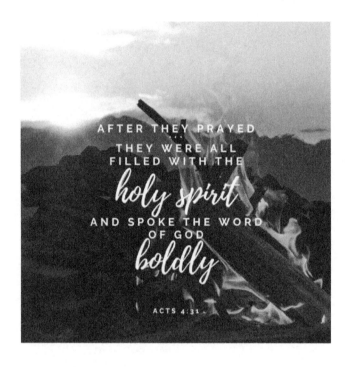

The Holy Spirit who makes us bold

 By Patricia Royston

Now, Lord, ... enable your servants to speak your word with great boldness. Stretch out your hand to heal and perform signs and wonders through the name of your holy servant Jesus.

After they had prayed, ... they were all filled with the Holy Spirit and spoke the word of God boldly.

Acts 4:29-31

I don't think there is a single one of us who would not have wanted to be around in those early days of the church, to witness what took place then ... to have seen tongues of fire come down upon those who were waiting, and to have heard those men speaking in the tongues (languages) of the foreigners living in their vicinity, sharing the gospel with power and hundreds receiving salvation immediately!

That must have been amazing!

Many of us dream about doing great exploits for God, don't we? I know I do!!

I often think on Jesus' words, *'... they will do even greater things than these .... You may ask me for anything in my name, and I will do it'* (John 14:12, 14).

How does that happen? How do we get to do those *'greater things'*, especially now in these days of a devastating pandemic?

This past year I have attended the Training for Supernatural Ministry [TSM] course at King's Arms Church in Bedford, where we are encouraged to be bold and (very) courageous, especially when we would go out onto the streets and into pubs on outreach!!! I find doing things like that quite nerve-wracking!!! However, to be able to step out in faith and confidence means spending time in the Father's presence and being filled and led by the Holy Spirit. Only then are we able to speak boldly, sharing the gospel and what God has impressed upon us, bringing insight and encouragement, truth, strength, peace, comfort and healing to those we meet, portraying God's love, grace and compassion. We're able to actively represent God's kingdom here on earth, as it is in heaven!

Let's take some time in the next few days to wait on the Lord and be of good courage, allowing Him to show us a colleague, neighbour or friend who He would like to bless with healing, encouragement and love at this time!

The Holy Spirit, our Comforter

By Gary Wood

I really enjoy cycling through our local countryside especially when it's warm and sunny, as it has been recently, exercising and being recharged by the beauty of God's creation. This time is also a good time to pray, either stopping to do so or as I ride.

Whilst out recently, I came across a police roadblock following a motorcycle accident and as I often do, I found myself praying for the rider and the other people involved, praying for them to receive God's supernatural comfort.

For the people involved, this accident could be a life changing event and for all of us, life sometimes takes an unexpected direction and we might find ourselves in a 'new normal' through illness or a major trauma. Amid these situations we might feel that God is distant, or our prayers are unanswered, and this can be a test of our faith.

It got me thinking about how the Holy Spirit provides us with truths, revealed through scripture that we can call on for comfort, truths that shape our worldview and whilst not necessarily bringing physical comfort these truths can strengthen us in our faith and our ability to keep on believing and to go on being transformed.

In Paul's letter to the **Philippians**, he writes in **chapter 3 verse 20** that 'Our citizenship is in heaven,' and this passage reminds us that this life is transitory, we're just passing through because we're waiting for our bodies to be transformed and for us to inhabit the new heaven and new earth, to be in God's presence as described in the final chapters of Revelation.

This is our hope, this is our anchor, this is our comfort and as Paul continues, 'We eagerly await a saviour from there [Heaven], the Lord Jesus Christ, who by the power that enables him to bring everything under his control, will transform our lowly bodies so that they will be like his glorious body.'

The Holy Spirit who leads us

By Jean Eames

And I will ask the Father, and he will give you another Counsellor to be with you forever – the Spirit of truth. The world cannot accept him, because it neither sees him nor knows him. But you know him, for he lives with you and will be in you. **John 14:16-17**

Paul asked them, "Did you receive the Holy Spirit when you believed?"

They answered, *"No, we have not even heard that there is a Holy Spirit."* (Acts 19:2)

I became a Christian when I was quite young and was baptised aged 14. We did preparation classes and I was a very enthusiastic young Christian during the Billy Graham crusades in London. But if you had asked me the question Paul posed the disciples he found in Ephesus, my answer might not have been so very different from theirs. Of course I knew vaguely about the Holy Spirit, but not in practise in my own life; He was usually referred to as It, not He. He certainly wasn't One to whom we addressed our prayers!

Then came the era known as 'The Movement of the Holy Spirit', in the 1970s when Brian and I were living in Ampthill, parents of young children. A Mission took place in Ampthill Park and because our children were too young to be left alone, we took it in turns to attend the meetings. There, our eyes were opened and we learned so much more about the Person and work of the Holy Spirit. He became a real Person to me, one to whom I could pray – no longer 'It', but 'He'. We welcomed Him into our lives. Such joy and exhilaration! No more blinkers on when I read the Bible, suddenly seeing His influence in aspect after aspect in His Word.

Verse 6 in this chapter tells us that, *"When Paul placed his hands on them, the Holy Spirit came on them and they spoke in other tongues and prophesied."* We have just had Pentecost Sunday in the Church calendar, when we remember the Christian church's birthday, for which we give praise and thanks. I praise God I no longer think, *"No, we have not even heard that there is a Holy Spirit"* and that we now acknowledge Him and give Him His rightful place.

Rest

By Steph Phillips

If I'm honest I find "rest" a challenge, and if I'm being truthful sometimes my "busyness" can overstep and become my identity. I'm sometimes guilty of having the mindset of "fast is good, slow is bad."

So in this season, there has been a growing whisper, enforced by the impact of lockdown, to take a deeper look at God's perspective on the subject.

In the beginning ...

> *By the seventh day God had finished the work . On the seventh day he rested from all his work.*
> **Genesis 2:2**

In the past, when I've read this verse I've just "skipped" over it, not really being intentional about really absorbing and noticing it. **God rested from all his work.**

In John's Gospel, Jesus talks about "the way" to the Father being through Him. I'm beginning to realise that Jesus' lifestyle, that is His "way", would also include rest. His Father commanded it in the form of Sabbath rest.

So what does that really mean? Why did Father God choose to make rest part of creation and commanded us to do so too? More importantly, if, as a Christian, I believe that the Bible is a blueprint for living the best life possible what am I doing about it? The whisper has now grown too loud to ignore.

There have been a couple of times in my life where I have been forced to rest from everything quite dramatically, which at that time was a huge inconvenience. However, it has been through those places of enforced REST that I have found most restoration and healing.

I'm not a fan of dramatic stops, so in this season I have been reading John Mark Comer's "Ruthless Elimination of Hurry" (which I highly recommend). I've found it a real challenge, particularly the chapters on the Sabbath and making this a lifestyle - I'm working on it!

One thing though I do know, rest brings me healing and restoration. This in turn brings me greater freedom which ultimately allows me to shine more effectively for Him, and that is something I want to pursue.

Journeying

By John and Cherry Parkinson

(with South Sudanese fishing spears in the background!)

We are all on a unique journey now, not on a terrestrial one but on a spiritual journey. Although our eventual destination is clear and confirmed our immediate journey is not so defined for many around world.

> *Trust in the Lord with all your heart, and lean not on your own understanding. In all your ways acknowledge Him and He will direct your paths.*
> **Proverbs 3:5**

Cherry and I have found this very reassuring and encouraging in some really challenges times in the past. Life is full of challenges and uncertain times, and faith in our Lord's protection and direction has seen us through some really difficult times. We have found this numerous times and in a number of different locations including and perhaps especially when living and working among people of other faiths as well as cultures.

At the start of our life's journey together we thought that we would be living in rural Zimbabwe in an environment that we loved and that we knew well. This was not to be and when we moved to the UK and were first posted back to Africa, this time to the Nubba Mountains in SW Sudan, we faced some very challenging situations. Whilst we were aware on several occasions of having guardian angels watching over us, looking back we were aware in our time in Sudan and subsequently in remote places of God's leading and protection.

Right now, we are all on a journey and some will be wondering where they will be after this present Covid-19 hiatus is over. Be assured that our Lord is guarding over you and he will guide all of us safely to calmer waters.

Fear not, I am with you, be note dismayed for I am your God. I will strengthen you. Yes, I will help you. I will uphold you with my righteous hand.
Isaiah 41:10

HOPE, a poem

By Carolyn Chappell

In July 2008, on one of my trips to Peterborough Cathedral – I lived in Peterborough for 10 years prior coming to Ampthill and had some of my most treasured times as a nurse in that lovely city – this beautiful prayer was written on a flipchart in the porch for everyone to read as they entered. If you take the first letter of each line in each verse, they spell HOPE.

Hope in the place of discord,
Opportunities out of challenges,
Praise instead of criticism,
Encouragement to replace despair.

Holiness and wholeness,
One purpose for many people,
Prayer that leads to action,
Everyone finding a place to belong.

Healing for those who are broken,
Order out of chaos,
Protection for the vulnerable,
Enterprise for all.

Health of body, mind and spirit,
Open hearted attitudes,
Passion for justice and mercy,
Expectations and visions fulfilled.

(author unknown)

In these very challenging and devastating times of today, I feel that there is so much in these beautiful lines. They spell out the clear message of HOPE that must surely be deep within our hearts and verse 3 seems particularly relevant. Perhaps when we are through all of this, the world will be a kinder, less cynically cold place; a world where we can ALL live in tolerance and mutual respect; a world where peace is built with justice and justice is guided by love. Every time I see a rainbow with its clear and powerful message of a promise, I know that our Lord IS with us.

> *But let justice roll down like the waters and*
> *righteousness like an ever-flowing stream.*
> **Amos 5:24**

God's unlikely choices

By Lesley Taaffe

Out of the strong came something sweet. **Judges 14:14**

I've been reading a book by Jeff Lucas called "There Are No Strong People" which encourages us by looking at the life of Samson. Now I have to admit that Samson has got to be one of my least favourite Bible characters. His petulant arrogance, his cruelty to both humans and animals and his hypocrisy of being a man of God (a Nazirite, no less!) and yet consorting with a prostitute has often made me question his inclusion in the Sacred Text as any sort of an example.

But that's our God for you. The Bible is full of inadequate, flawed, sinful people. Just like the people who read the scriptures.

God's word is no fairy story. Sometimes it's a hard read with it's frank speech and warts-and-all narratives of characters and events. It is an account of how a Perfect God works in an imperfect world. He is God. He does not need us to help him fulfil his purposes. And yet (wonder of wonders) he CHOOSES to call us and use us, no matter who or what we are. God can use anyone to work for good, to spread the Good News of his salvation and power, even the most flawed of individuals – and Samson certain sits firmly in that category; even as I do.

It's easy to read the Bible account of some people - Samson (arrogant), King David (adulterer and murderer), Jonah (coward), to name but a few – and judge them, to wonder how on earth God could deal with such dreadful people and put them in the Bible as examples to us.

But they are in the Bible for a reason. They were real, flesh and blood people whom God used for his purposes. And in part they are there as a mirror to our own inadequacies and failings. But not just that – God is too loving to just hold a mirror up to our weaknesses – they are there to show that God loves us all, no matter who or what we are. He knows us inside and out, there is nothing hidden from him, not even our darkest thoughts. And yet with all that intimate and uncomfortable knowledge, still he calls us to be in fellowship with him. Like the father in the story of the Prodigal Son, he stands staring down the road waiting, longing, for his son – us – to come home to him, to accept his forgiveness and to be wrapped in the cloak of his love that blots out our weaknesses and failings and, through the power of the cross, transforms us into children of God.

I can't say I've come away from Jeff's book liking Samson much more than I did before I read it. But I am less judgemental of him. And I am filled with even greater appreciation for the truly immense love of God. I suffer (as many of us do) from feelings of inadequacy and self-doubt. But reading the account of Samson has shown me just how powerful God's love is, how inclusive and forgiving it is. And it is there for ALL of us.

It is indeed Amazing Grace that can save even a wretch like me.

And a final scripture to ponder: Psalm 103:8-12

*The L*ORD *is compassionate and gracious,*
slow to anger, abounding in love.
He will not always accuse,
nor will he harbor his anger forever;
he does not treat us as our sins deserve
or repay us according to our iniquities.
For as high as the heavens are above the earth,
so great is his love for those who fear him;
as far as the east is from the west,
so far has he removed our transgressions from us.

Amen.

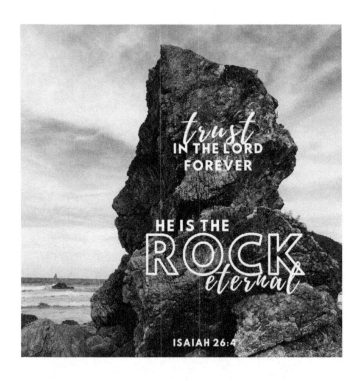

Smoke in your eyes?

By Ken Argent

Though I am like a wineskin in the smoke, I do not forget your decrees.
Psalm 119:83

If wineskins could talk, this one might have said:

"Once I was in daily use but now I'm forgotten; once I had a special place at family celebrations but now I'm lonely and of little value: once everyone loved me but now I'm forgotten; once I was supple leather but now hanging up here in the rafters the smoky fire has made me dry and useless ..."

The writer of Psalm 119 looked up one day at a wineskin hanging in the roof of his ancient home, where the smoke of the fire had no way of escape but to swirl around the discarded wineskin, and the psalmist said, "that is how I feel today – dry, forgotten, devalued, lonely, and useless."

Whether we be young or older there are times when we too may sometimes feel the same – particularly in lockdown circumstances.

But – and it is an important but ... the Psalmist resolved to remember God's word because God always values us; never forgets us; can always use us; and his word always guides us in the right and best direction.

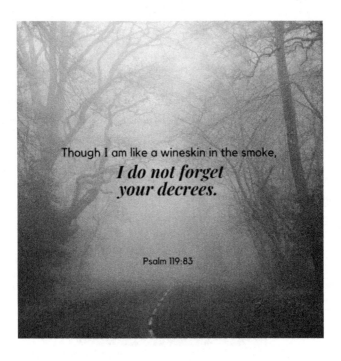

Though I am like a wineskin in the smoke,
I do not forget
your decrees.

Psalm 119:83

Courage

By Ruth Baker

The LORD is with me; I will not be afraid. What can man do to me? **Psalm 118:6**

I think of courage as being brave and stepping out of our comfort zone.

But what's the point? Why do something we don't like doing? As a Christian, it is God-given courage that enables me to step out in faith, and allow others to see, know, or experience the love of God.

In my second year of university, I felt it was right to take on the hard role of leading what was an almost non-existent Christian Union. This was not easy at first, and I found it discouraging at times, and I wanted to give up and let someone else do it.

Someone from my university church gave me these words of encouragement:

"You feel you're in a dark room with just a small flame, yet even that small flame can light up that dark room. Do not be overwhelmed. God is with you and goes before you."

This encouragement is that by having courage and stepping out, we can be lighting up our work-place, our friendship groups, and our community. The light of Christ living in us and being on display can lead others to see and know God. All of a sudden there is so much reason to step out and do something brave. Step out and love radically, for the salvation of others.

And the greatest encouragement for me when stepping out is from Psalm 118:6, "God is on my side".

THE LORD IS WITH ME; I WILL NOT BE AFRAID. WHAT CAN MAN DO TO ME?

PSALM 118:6

Meekness

By Geoff Richardson

Regaining strength within the word 'meek': it is not weak!

Blessed are the meek for they will inherit the earth. **Matthew 5:5**

In the 1970s I was attending a student weekend at Lee Abbey, in north Devon, led by Jonathan Lamb (our local UCCF representative in Exeter) and the Beatitudes were a focus for our study.

I'd grown up with Ladybird book images of a Jesus that very much fitted the words "Gentle Jesus, Meek and Mild ..." and now, as a bloke who played sport and inhabited the world of Engineering Science, I found this image very inadequate in fitting my heartfelt expectation ... of the character of the carpenter's son from Galilee who commanded the respect of tough Galilean fishermen.

Jonathan Lamb explained that the Greek word for 'meek' (*praus*) was far from weak and was used to define the quality of the chariot horse running on the inside of the stadium's circuit. Meekness here is defining controlled power as opposed to unbridled power! Power that responds to the charioteer's command through his use of the rein, shout or other device.

Jesus' first cousin, the apostle and disciple John, brother of James (sons of Salome and Zebedee) reports within his Gospel that Jesus was doing His Father's works. He was meekly obeying the Father's "reign"... if you'll excuse the pun.

If you have time do please read these crucial paragraphs: John 5:36-44, 7:14-17, 17:1-11. Unlike us, Jesus' priority was never self!

We can thus imagine ourselves teamed up in harness with the lead Horse, Jesus – discipleship is all about learning from Him – and obeying the Father's command that His will be done on earth. Jesus never doubted His Father's love and gave himself utterly to God's cause of redeeming us, dealing justly with the source of evil and graciously with the consequence of evil for us, upon the cross. What a powerful image of meekness, especially with the evil taunts from those mocking him!

Graham Kendrick's words of the song "Meekness & Majesty" have for me supplanted the wishy-washy words of my youth. How do you think of meekness?

Meekness is not weakness for we are empowered by the same Spirit that raised Jesus from the dead. So, today as we go about our lives (in the somewhat weird routines that our Government's response to Coronavirus has demanded of us), will we act from self-interest or in fulfilling the calling we have as children of God's family?

Our security

By George Banks

We have this hope as an anchor to the soul, firm and secure ....
Hebrews 6:19

I suppose we all feel a little insecure at times, especially as things are at present. Over the last few years I have become more and more aware of my physical vulnerability. Several times I have slipped on a ladder and just the other day I had a fall when the stool I was standing on slipped from under me, while I was trying to undo a screw in an awkward position. I ended up with a black eye from the screwdriver (and if anyone should see me, that's my story, it's nothing to do with Crystal).

An anchor is a very good symbol of security. But the thing about anchors, for it to do it's job, it has to be fixed to something that won't move. When we were sailing on the broads we had what was called a mud anchor, for obvious reasons, which was fine generally, but it would drift in the mud in strong winds. Many of us are going through tough times at the moment, and things we have depended on have been a bit insecure: jobs, finances, loss of family and friends, and life has changed, even meeting up together.

Our text speaks of an anchor which goes right into the sanctity which is the very heart of God because Jesus is there, on our behalf.

When we give our lives to Jesus, He provides us with the anchor, which is safely secured in Jesus by our Saviour's love, and we have this promise from God that it cannot be moved (verses 17 and 18). The point about this is, it's a bit like lock-down, we cannot see Him but we know He's there. In the same way we can speak to Him at all times and find comfort and reassurance. We just have to do it.

If I had considered health and safety when I was standing on my stool I would have asked Crystal to put her foot on it to make it secure. God is way ahead of us with health and safety, He had his foot on the stool from the beginning, and our confidence in Him is secure. I have a black eye to remind me!

WE HAVE THIS
HOPE
AS AN
anchor FOR THE soul

Hebrews 6:19

A humble attitude

 By Bernard Coen

I've been struggling recently with my reaction to seeing statues being toppled and what ordinary people are saying about it. Some things I've seen and read are so full of passion that they have been interpreted as aggressive by others (including me). I've seen a very small number of people, citing failures in the justice system, proposing their own rough justice. And I've been scared by the backlash I have witnessed (sometime in places I did not expect to find it). I've seen a very small number using this opportunity to justify violence. There is no doubting the passion on display, which seems to push people into opposing camps on a variety of related issues. But what should a Christian do? We could stop watching the news but that does not stop us knowing there is sadness and tension in the world.

Recently I've been finding wisdom in the Bible that helps me when I am speaking with others about current polarising topics. The first letter of Peter was written to believers and focuses a lot on how they should relate to and deal with each other. For example, in **1 Peter 3:8-9** we read,

> *Finally, all of you should be of one mind. Sympathize with each other. Love each other as brothers and sisters. Be tenderhearted, and keep a humble attitude. Don't repay evil for evil. Don't retaliate with insults when people insult you. Instead, pay them back with a blessing.* (New Living Translation)

I've been bearing this in mind when dealing with non-believers, whose passion has led them to express themselves in ways I don't really understand or would not express myself. I pray that the Holy Spirit will enable me to hold back on voicing what might look like justice to me and instead give me the humility to try to understand them more, to try to sympathise, but most of all to be 'tenderhearted' to people feeling stung into passionate action.

And I pray that the Holy Spirit will help me to express these verses with a humble attitude in the hope that the people I'm speaking to might see the wisdom in it.

River of prayer

By Maryla Carter

When you pass through the waters, I will be with you; and when you pass through the rivers, they will not sweep over you. **Isaiah 43:2a**

Praying, it has been said, can feel like using a telephone on a faulty line and struggling to get through to God. But it needn't be that way.

One sunny morning in June 1972, I rose shortly after dawn, in the foothills of the French Pyrenees, and set off before breakfast to climb a particular peak which had caught my eye on the previous day. As a teenager without a map, I was unprepared when I discovered that a swiftly flowing river lay between myself and my goal, which rose up majestically across the waters, beckoning me on. Alas, there was no sign of a bridge. But for me, giving up was not an option!

And so I promptly jumped into the river, fully clothed, in order to swim across. The moment that my body got caught up in the swirling waters, I realised that I had committed an act of extreme folly. So strong was the current, that any thoughts of getting *across* the river were instantly replaced by my desperate attempts to simply get *out* of the river. By the grace of God, I survived – although totally drenched!

Fast forward some 48 years to April 2020. I'm sitting in our cosy bed at home, reading a book about prayer by the recently deceased Anglican bishop Simon Barrington-Ward. Barrington-Ward dismissed the faulty telephone-line model of prayer and then, to my utter astonishment and delight, suggested that we could think of prayer as **plunging into a river,** and being carried along – swimming in a current which, on account of the prayers of others, is already moving. How easily I can relate to this!

Through this metaphor I am gaining new perspectives on prayer. I'm learning to trust that the journey on which the river takes me is better than simply staying on the river-bank, that is, not daring to pray at all. Or, when praying becomes tough due to God's apparent silence, I might even be tempted to thrash my way to the river bank, rather than remain in the river, trustingly, until God carries me to *His* desired destination.

Plunging into God's River enables us to make meaningful progress in life. It is not an act of folly, but of wisdom itself.

Solitude

By Alex Vickers

But Jesus would often go to some place where he could be alone and pray. **Luke 5:16**

As we begin to emerge from lockdown it may seem a strange time to think about solitude. For most people this is a time to escape confinement and enjoy the things that have been denied for the last few months. Solitude is different to isolation though; isolation is something imposed by things outside our control. It may be a virus, as we have all experienced, it may be through circumstance – losing loved ones through bereavement or by moving job or house. Isolation can mean loneliness and the loss of joy that can bring. Solitude, however, is something we choose for ourselves. It is interwoven through scripture and was commonplace in the life of those who followed God closely – no more so than Jesus, who went to "lonely places" to spend time in quietness with his Father. It is a place to hear from God, our loving Father and to encounter again the Holy Spirit. It is a place to recover strength and joy.

In After 8's we have been looking at spiritual disciplines and how by using them we can deepen our faith and relationship with God. Solitude is one such discipline. For some it is easier than others – for someone with ADHD sitting quietly in a dark room alone would be torture. It isn't the place or the process though. It is to still our minds, even if we can only do this by keeping our bodies busy. It is to centre our thoughts on Jesus, to give him space to speak to us. We may need to keep re-centring our thoughts on Him when other thoughts invade. I often have trouble hearing from God, but like trying to listen to a Zoom meeting when everyone is speaking we need to be quiet sometimes and listen. Let's leave our screens behind and give God space to speak to us. Why not try it for 2 minutes and see how it goes? God is waiting to speak with us, sometimes He just needs us to listen.

BUT JESUS OFTEN WITHDREW TO *lonely places* AND PRAYED.

LUKE 5:16

How long, Lord, how long?

By Andy Harris

We have known many types of longing through the last few months, from longing for a haircut to longing for safety and freedom from fear of an invisible virus.

We went for a walk in a wood a month ago and Kym took some photos. On looking at one photo of me, I was intrigued by the question of "How long?"

I first thought of David in the Psalms. David is linked with just under half of the 150 psalms, and over one third of the 150 psalms are petitions for help, including many of David's. The apostle Paul described David as "a man after God's own heart" in Acts 13:22-23. David, the man of God, was free in expression of his longings to God, and trusting that God would answer.

My soul is in anguish. How long, O LORD, how long?
Psalm 6:3

Then I looked at other perspectives of longing.

Romans 8:19-21 says that 'For the creation waits in eager expectation for the children of God to be revealed .... in hope that the creation itself will be liberated from its bondage to decay and brought into the freedom and glory of the children of God.'

Jesus longed for people to have faith (Mark 9:19) and longed that He could gather the people together in His safe keeping, but they would not come (Luke 13:34). The apostle Peter writes that 'The Lord is not slow in keeping his promise, as some understand slowness. Instead he is patient with you, not wanting anyone to perish, but everyone to come to repentance.' (2 Peter 3:9)

When we hesitate to trust God with our deepest longings and try to cope on our own, we step back from God's grace. All our longings that come from us being God's children, are longings that look to God for fulfilment, and they find corresponding longings from God for us.

I want to trust God more and I want to jump into that river of prayer (described by Maryla a few days ago).

I also want a haircut.

And to finish:

> Let us then approach God's throne of grace with confidence, so that we may receive mercy and find grace to help us in our time of need. **Hebrews 4:16**

Gratitude

By Claudia Tyson

Give thanks, in all circumstances.
1 Thessalonians 5:18

A week or two after the challenge of Covid-19 hit our land, someone suggested we should unite in showing gratitude to our NHS by standing on doorsteps each Thursday evening and applauding. This very quickly became the thing to do. TV cameras filmed and pictures were live-streamed of people in all parts of the country, at ambulance stations, fire stations, offices, countryside and in cities, joining together to say "Thank you." Rainbows appeared in many windows with the words 'Thank you NHS' written beneath; even arches of rainbow coloured balloons over one house in Ampthill!

Initially some of us working in the NHS felt slightly embarrassed. We are just doing the jobs we are paid to do. Nothing special really. One of my colleagues complained that she would prefer people to be grateful to us all the time, not just on a Thursday evening in a national health crisis, when "they make a lot of noise and wake up my sleeping children!"

'Please' and 'Thank you' are words that we expect

parents to teach their children as soon as they can speak, yet in much of today's society they are hardly spoken. How important is it as we go about our daily lives that we show an example of gratitude for all that others do for us, however small. When did you last say 'thank you' to the men emptying the dustbins or the cleaners at the supermarket, getting on with their jobs often unnoticed? When did you last write a thank you letter? Or send a text to express your gratitude for an unexpected kindness?

The Message (2 Corinthians 9) speaks of showing our gratitude through our offerings for and care for our needy brothers and sisters – donations as thank offerings.

One suggestion, made by some learned psychologist, for everyone to get through the lockdown was to write down 3 things each day to be thankful for. But they didn't suggest who one should be thankful to? We are assured that our heavenly Father is the one who gives good things to us. How much we have to thank God for! Let's thank Him daily for each and every blessing, big and small, show our gratitude through our actions and be prepared to explain the reason for our thankfulness.

Thanks be to God for his indescribable gift!
2 Corinthians 9:15

Growth

By Catherine Sleight

Jesus says, *"Remain in me and I will remain in you. No branch can bear fruit by itself; it must remain in the vine."* **John 15:4**

When I was first approached to write a Thought for the Day, I didn't really know what to write, then I heard yesterday that Bob had passed away, following a long-term illness. I have known Bob all my life, he was my friend's dad, much loved and will be much missed.

One of my enduring memories of him (apart from the fantastic parties and games he used to organise for our church family!) was that he was one of my Sunday School teachers. Along with many others before and since, he was able to encourage me in my walk with God, helping me increase my Bible knowledge through stories and the Sword Drill(!), but also teaching me about God's love, encouraging me to pray, and being a Christian role model. Moving my faith from a head-knowledge to a heart-knowledge of God's love for me and Jesus' willing sacrifice so that I could be part of God's family. In later years, I also worked alongside him, teaching in the Junior Church and encouraging other children and young people in their faith.

Faith is a lifelong journey, and we should always try to keep growing in God. In life we will face many challenges, but if we are rooted in God's word, in Christ's love, we can stand firm. We can also know that there is a network of other Christians around us, other branches, praying and encouraging us and helping us grow. Especially when we are struggling. That's not something I'd considered until now!

I can be quite poor at self-discipline, and certainly when it comes to spending personal time with God. In this time of Coronavirus I have valued even more the contact with other Christians through livestream services, Homegroup meetings on Zoom, and Christian friends and family who try to keep me honest in my faith and encourage me to keep growing.

I will miss Bob. But I will also choose to thank God for his life as he has helped me to grow in faith. So...

- Who can you thank God for today – who has introduced you to God for the first time, who has challenged you to think more deeply about your faith, who has helped you to know God's love?

- How can you keep growing in God, who can help you with this?

- Who can you encourage and support in their faith, to help them grow?

May God bless you now and always, Catherine xxx

More than Conquerors

By Michael Mead

No, in all things we are more than conquerors through him who loved us.
Romans 8:37

Do you have a favourite chapter in the Bible? Or perhaps you have several favourites – or your favourite might change with the seasons of faith, or life's experiences. One of my favourite chapters has always been Romans 8, as it's overflowing with amazing biblical truths and reassuring promises. Written by Paul to the fledgling church in the heart of the Roman Empire, this chapter is brimming with encouragement and certainty, whatever present sufferings (v.8) the believers are facing.

Paul reminds the believers, and us, that 'in all things God works for the good of those who love him and have been called according to his purpose' (v.28). He then follows that with two amazing lists of the things that **cannot** separate us from the love of Christ (v.35 and vv.38-39). Trouble, hardship, persecution, famine, nakedness, danger, sword, death nor life, angels nor demons, the present nor the future, any powers, neither height nor depth nor anything else in all creation. Well – that covers most things I experience at home in Ampthill and at work in Milton Keynes! Hidden in between these two lists is verse 37 – 'No, in all these things we are **more than conquerors** through him who loved us.' Not *just* conquerors, but **more than** conquerors – how encouraging is that!

You may not need to conquer famine this week, or conquer persecution next week. I'm not expecting to face the sword imminently or nakedness anytime soon. So – is this relevant to 21st century Bedfordshire residents? Of course it is – because the things we need to conquer daily are just as important to our loving God. Perhaps just getting out of bed is your mountain every day, or overcoming your eating disorder, or facing unemployment, or talking civilly to your family/ neighbour/work colleague, or controlling your finances, or not drinking or gambling, or coping with loneliness, or staying faithful to your partner, or keeping your social media controlled and keeping the integrity of the content you post – or any other of the myriad of things we experience daily. Paul reminds us – that as believers, with God's power and grace – we can be 'more than conquerors' of any or all these things.

Hospitality

 By Tim Darby (with BMS World Mission in Gulu, Uganda)

Faith in Christ, Abundant life: We're an evangelical mission agency transforming the lives of people in fragile states and under-evangelised communities, among the world's most marginalised people, on four continents. www.bmsworldmission.org

ABC have had links with BMS over many years and we currently partner with the Darby family in Gulu, Uganda, and with Annie Tanner in Kathmandu, Nepal. Tim works to support communities to provide a clean, secure and sustainable water supply and Linda is a lawyer involved in training and education to combat gender violence and to enhance safeguarding practices.

....

Classical hospitality is something many of us have not been practicing during 2020 for obvious reasons and many of us will be keen to start again. There is a good reason for this; it is a biblical principle, ingrained in the Old Testament culture as a 'good' and instructed about in the New Testament. Interestingly the Bible instructs us to be ready to both give and receive hospitality. For example, **Romans 12:13** *'When God's people are in need, be ready to help them. Always be eager to practice hospitality.'* And **Matthew 10:10b** *"Don't hesitate to accept hospitality, because those who work deserve to be fed."* (both NLT)

Here in northern Uganda, the principles and practices of hospitality are heavily ingrained in the culture and I think we have a lot to learn from the people. During the last few months three of the eight young men who work with WET Consulting (a business as mission venture set up by BMS) became fathers for the first time. It is usual here for everyone who knows the parents to visit the new family so when lockdown restrictions allowed, I went to see them. As customary, I took a few basics for the house (flour, sugar, soap, etc.) and then, as a more western custom, some baby things our children had grown out of. I had thought I was coming to greet them, bless them and bring them gifts but like the three wise men the visitors received a greater blessing than the gift-bearers. I travelled along with two others of the team to the home village and was greeted like family by the whole wider family and, despite only an hour's notice of our coming, a full chicken dinner!

I did not hesitate to accept (after all, it's biblical!) but more importantly I have been challenged to improve my own hospitality efforts. I wonder how we can all be eager and creative in helping God's people in need during this current climate?

The Power of the Cross

By Jane Spencer

> *"If anyone would come after me, let him deny himself and take up his cross and follow me."*
> **Matthew 16:24**

What have you been reading this summer; a biography, a historical novel, a chic lit romance or maybe a Sci-Fi mystery?

Some of us are avid readers of crime books. For me the interest in these books lies in the interplay between the contrasting characters of the Detective Inspector and their Detective Sergeant, and in the geographical location of the book. These take precedent over the actual crime committed. This summer two different series set in Northumberland and a new series set in the Dee Valley caught my attention. I enjoy the locations so much I even have my own mental crime book map of the UK!

On finishing the last book my thoughts then turned to what was apparently the greatest crime in history: the crucifixion of Christ. The location: a skull shaped hill, a torture site on a hillside in Israel; the key characters: the chief priests of Jerusalem, a Roman Emperor, a baying crowd, a group of followers, a traitor, a murderer, and a carpenter from Bethlehem; the evidence: eyewitness accounts, Old Testament references, and then details of the horrific nature of the crime itself.

As a young enquirer into what Christians believe, many had discussed with me endlessly about what Jesus did and what he taught. However it was not until the crucifixion and the meaning of the cross was preached, did it suddenly make sense to me why a response was required. 'Sitting on the fence' was an inadequate response. The choice was stark; either you walked away from what Jesus' death on the cross signified, or you walked towards the cross knowing that the suffering and sacrifice Jesus made was personal, given to redeem you. Only when I was led to truly grasp the nature and meaning of Jesus' sacrifice did I place my life in God's hands.

These remain the only two choices. The offer remains on the table, written in four different Gospel accounts. If you decide not to accept then you walk away and the crucifixion remains as just a terrible act, a crime set in a dramatic location with key characters to hold your attention, as in a work of fiction. To accept, you take up your own cross and follow Jesus.

- We need to pray particularly for our young people to understand the significance and power of the cross.

- We need to have asked them about the choice they have made which will have a profound impact on how they lead their lives (particularly if they are going into a new workplace now, or away to university this term when every other intellectual, faith and lifestyle offer will be put in front of them).

- As we move ahead from the lockdown experience what does the cross still demand of each of us today? As a 'seasoned' Christian, do I retain that awareness of the enormity of the cross and do I retain discipline in prayer to listen to what God is asking me to do with my life each day because of Christ's sacrifice?

- Is the cross still a life-changing choice, or am I in danger of letting it become a piece of fiction?

And finally, a song which reflects on the cross:

https://www.youtube.com/watch?v=nPFv-ywTY-c

('The Power of the Cross', by Stuart Townend)

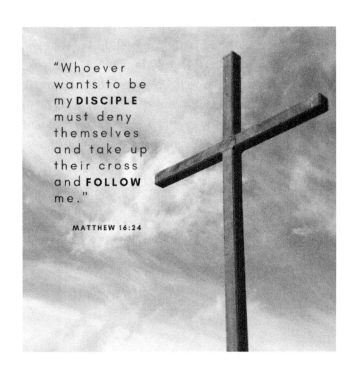

"Whoever wants to be my **DISCIPLE** must deny themselves and take up their cross and **FOLLOW** me."

MATTHEW 16:24

God is love

By Ian Horsler

And so we know and rely on the love God has for us. God is love. Whoever lives in love lives in God, and God in him.
1 John 4:16

Sometimes, I'm sure, at school we were asked to write a precis – perhaps reducing two thousand words to one hundred. What if we had to write a precis of the Bible? I think the Beloved Disciple achieved it.

In 1878, Cleopatra's Needle, which Moses would have seen, was brought to London from Egypt. It hadn't been moved for nearly 2000 years, and it was decided to put a time capsule underneath to surprise anybody else who moved it. Along with coins, newspapers, photos of Queen Victoria and some beautiful women, they put the Bible and John 3 verse 16 in 215 languages – "For God so loved the world that He gave His only begotten Son, that whosoever believeth in Him should not perish, but have everlasting life". (They didn't have NIV!) The Gospel in a nutshell.

But suppose we have to be more economical with words – we're only allowed three! In his first letter, John again gives it – GOD IS LOVE – does that sum up the Bible? If you had to complete GOD IS ...... what would you put? We could say Power, Wisdom, Beauty, Justice, but above all He is LOVE. It's a message that is not just found in the Bible, but in all the varied experiences of life! In 55 years of marriage, Chris and I have found continually that He is love. We've seen countless wonders of creation, stood where Livingstone stood when he first saw the Victoria Falls. As we look at our children, grandchildren and great grandchildren, who can doubt that GOD IS LOVE?

But wait! 2020 makes us doubt, doesn't it? In this awful pandemic, can we really say that God is love? Suffering seems to deny it, doesn't it? "Why? Why?", we say. An old hymn says, "I am not skilled to understand what God hath willed, what God hath planned – I only know at His right hand stands One who is my Saviour."

Years ago, young ladies used to sew samplers and bookmarks, and a popular choice of words was GOD IS LOVE (cos it's short!) One side was perfect and lovely, but look at the reverse – it's a tangle of threads – just like coronavirus.

But it's supremely as we look at the cross that we wonder and adore. Thomas Kelly wrote, "Inscribed upon the cross we see in shining letters – GOD IS LOVE."

He is our Creator God ... He cares for us.

by Gill Rowe

When I first moved to Ampthill 25 years ago, I was thrilled to discover, at the top of Ampthill Park looking over a fantastic view, a plaque with Psalm 8 written on it.

> 'Lord, our Lord, how majestic is your name in all the earth!
> You have set your glory in the heavens ...
> When I consider your heavens, the work of your fingers, the moon and the stars, which you have set in place,
> what is mankind that you are mindful of them, human beings that you care for them?'

This speaks of God the all-powerful Creator and His care for us, His most precious creation.

Over the last few decades(!) I have had the privilege of being able to travel both home and abroad, and have seen some spectacular sights. I have been to the Alps on several occasions, and the sight of the snow-capped mountain ranges never fails to take my breath away – wow! This, surely, is a display of God's majesty and power.

Just look around you and wonder at God's creation: its vastness, the variety, mystery, colours, imagination, humour, ingenuity and science, with its intricacy and interdependence. These things speak to me of a Creator God – in control, not out of control.

During this pandemic, I have struggled like many people have. I have been frustrated by my own weakness and inadequacy to cope with change of routines, freedoms, thwarted plans and uncertainty.

Has my faith been shaken? No. I am trusting that Creator God is in control, that He cares for me and that He will lead me to a fresh appreciation of Him, that He is bigger than all my earthly concerns.

So who is the God that you put your trust in, the all-powerful Creator God who cares for **you?**

Psalm 95 invites us to worship the Creator God:

> *... For the LORD is the great God... in His hand are the depths of the Earth, and the mountain peaks belong to Him. The sea is His, for He made it... for He is our God... we are the flock under His care.*
> **Psalm 95:3-5, 7**

Shout for joy and make music

By Gez Downing

'Shout for joy to the Lord, all the earth, burst into jubilant song with music; make music to the Lord with the harp, with the harp and the sound of singing.' **Psalm 98:4-5**

Music has always been a means of expressing one's feelings in an extremely visceral way. We see this especially in the Bible through the Psalms, some of the most emotive and personal passages in the Bible. Some are written out of loneliness, some out of anger, but this one in particular is written out of happiness, out of an overflowing of joy and praise. It speaks of using the gift of music to lift up God's name, exclaiming it for all to hear.

The times we live in are full of sadness and loneliness that can easily drag us down and invade out hearts, and the pessimism of the world can so easily envelop our minds. It can sometimes be hard to be joyful and loud. But we have a reason to have that joy! Our joy comes from our knowledge of God's amazing works and his love for us. And this joy is like no other, it is not a worldly joy but a spiritual joy that can pierce into any situation, and there are beautiful ways in which God has given us to express this joy.

Through the gift of music, our joyful praise to God is not just a wonderful and creative way of worship, but also a means of reaching out to others. People feel music, and especially music with purpose. I have found that every non-Christian that I have brought along to a church event/Christian festival has come out of it and instantly commented on the music, and how it feels different. One of my housemates at University, who is not a believer, listens to worship music when he is stressed as it makes him feel a peace and a happiness that he finds in no other type of music. The music that flows from our worship has meaning, and people can feel that.

The gift of music, like so many other gifts that God has given us, are tools that we have been equipped with that allow us to express ourselves in ways that words cannot. And so, even though we cannot sing together in church at the moment, we will never lose this gift of music, we will always be able to sing God's praises and shout for joy.

Faith in action: what impact has Covid had on how we live?

By Simon Miller-Cranko

Jesus said, "'Love the Lord your God with all your passion and prayer and intelligence.' This is the most important, the first on any list. But there is a second to set alongside it: 'Love others as well as you love yourself.' These two commands are pegs; everything in God's Law and the Prophets hangs from them." **Matthew 22:37-40, from The Message**

What impact has Covid had on your faith? And what impact has your faith had on Covid?

In the days of Corona, during a time of catching up with a Christian friend, I was asked a hard question: "In the West, do we value life too highly?" After all, for many displaced families around the world, the covid-19 epidemic poses just another threat in a long line of hardships faced in everyday life. Whilst we isolate the infirm, suggesting gloves, masks and sanitiser for anyone who dare venture out despite being 2m apart, those in slums, refugee camps and war torn zones navigate life around cholera, malaria, dysentery, Ebola and trafficking as part of everyday life. Corona just becomes another bullet to dodge.

Will working from home, church on the telly and school by zoom be the new norm in a post-covid world? If the world has been so changed by the pandemic, how as Christians, has our response to the world changed? Are we still living inward-looking, self-preserving, pre-covid lives? Should we be supporting the same old charities striving to do the same old things or are there new opportunities to reach out to our neighbour?

Efforts to save lives and flatten the curve led to 81% of the global economy being shut down over the last few months. While this has saved many lives, it has also resulted in a global economic crisis on a scale we have not seen since World War II. The World Bank predicts a 5.2% contraction in the global economy this year and it is estimated that 34 million people will be pushed into extreme poverty in 2020 alone (people living on less than US$1.90 a day). Pre-covid, it was estimated that 40 million people were victims of modern slavery globally. Women, men, girls and boys living under the control of someone else, not free to leave, working for the benefit of others. Modern slavery happens in every country and is especially prevalent in our own backyard.

We are in this lake together, but on vastly different vessels. For the most vulnerable, already on a flimsy life raft, covid-19 has only made that more unstable.

Globally, World Vision International predicts that forced marriages will increase by an additional 13 million over next 10 years as families find themselves in cycles of debt to buy food after having eaten seed reserved for the 2020-21 crops. Forced labour is increasing globally and can be found in increasing child labour, excessive overtime, in migrant workers locked into factories or let go without pay, and in the production of face masks, gloves and other PPE, needed so urgently in our NHS. Modern slavery is already an almost invisible crime and with governments diverting many resources to covid responses, this crime has become even harder to detect.

As a people made in God's image, redeemed by Christ, living anew in the reality of the coming kingdom – what does good stewardship look like in my response to a post-covid world? How can my faith impact covid-19? Is it OK to contribute to the suffering of a fellow human being (also made in the image of God and loved by Him) because I am in need of virus protection?

Where I have been stopped in my tracks, should I begin to pick up from where I left off or, as lockdown restrictions are being lifted, should I be seeking a new opportunity to let my light shine?

Here are three opportunities you may wish to consider doing:

1) Commit to praying for God's protection on the newly "at-risk people" in Ampthill, whether that be through job loss, a feeling of entrapment and isolation, fear of the unknown, embarrassment of money worries, relationship breakdown and for victims of modern slavery locally and in the wider world.

2) Through the church, make use of the opportunities to support our local food bank, women's refuge and men's shelter or by calling in on or befriending a neighbour.

3) Be intentional in understanding the work of the Darby's, a missionary family whom we as a church support prayerfully and financially.

As God's people, can we individually consider prioritising the care of the vulnerable in our community? Isolated, unconnected individuals are at great risk of exploitation especially through social media and online scare-mongering. Are you able to stand with your Ampthill Baptist Church family, and continue to creatively reach out to all people, particularly those that have few safety nets.

Hidden treasure

By Cheryl Spicer

The parable of the hidden treasure:

The kingdom of heaven is like treasure hidden in a field. When a man found it, he hid it again, and then in his joy went and sold all he had and bought that field. **Matthew 13:44**

The reason I have chosen this parable is that it has shown me as I have been reading the Bible, Jesus has been my source of sustenance on a daily basis and I have felt God's presence strongly throughout these uncertain times we are currently facing. It has highlighted to me that it is only as we have an open heart and seek and search the scriptures that we gain wisdom, knowledge and understanding of God's provision and love for us.

What does treasure mean to you?

In Matthew 6 verse 21, Jesus says *"For where your treasure is, there your heart will be also."* Jesus wants to extract the hidden treasure within each one of us to fulfil our potential for His glory.

The parable of the hidden treasure illustrates that the hidden treasure Jesus is speaking about refers to the kingdom of Heaven that has everlasting value whereas treasure in the worldly realms refers to material items such as diamond rings, the latest gadget, expensive watches or an heirloom, which may give some sense of achievement or satisfaction, but are not everlasting and will eventually perish over time.

In this parable the man sells all that he owns. This reminds us and refers to Jesus who gave himself as the ultimate sacrifice and died for us in order that we may have life in all its fullness. The treasures represents us and the field represents the world. Jesus loves each one of us so much that we are God's treasure and precious in his eyes.

During these uncertain times it has taught me how to be still and focus on God, to be thankful for his unwavering love and sustenance and that He is the only source of contentment that worldly things cannot compare with.

May we each be a blessing to people through our behaviour and actions that people will see Christ in us and the love and hope that He gives us as we walk with Him.

God's good plans

By Jim Widdicks

"For I know the plans I have for you," declares the Lord, *"plans to prosper you and not to harm you, plans to give you hope and a future."*
Jeremiah 29:11

During my Christian life I have often struggled with things and questioned *WHY* would God allow *THAT* to happen. I am sure you can also think of things that cause you to ask the same question. Here are just a couple of examples that are very close to home for me.

A couple of years ago, Katrina, Bethany and I were introduced to Sabina, Zara and Zain. Sabina was very ill with Motor Neurone Disease and had just lost her husband Colin to a brain tumour. The whole family were intending to move to Marston to be closer to Colin's mother (Maureen) and stepfather (Alan) so that they could help out. Colin never made it, and Sabina only survived a few months after the move. Maureen and Alan attend Marston Vale Community Church and have since moved into Zara and Zain's house to look after them full time, not something they'd planned for their retirement.

Closer to home Katrina has lived with and suffered from M.E. for over 20 years now. This has a massive impact on not only her life, but also the lives of Bethany and me. When well, Trina led the 18-30 age youth group in our previous church and organised weekends away, Bible studies and led services. She then went away with YWAM to work in Bolivia with street children. It was during this time that Trina developed glandular fever which ultimately led to her developing M.E.

Finally, I don't know about you, but I have just about had it with Covid-19. I hate wearing a face mask when I do almost anything now and I simply want life to return to normal, the sooner the better as far as I'm concerned.

It's fair to say that the above examples would not have been what I wanted to happen. Happily, I am not in charge. I can often see good coming out of apparently bad things though. Colin and Sabina both became Christians and were baptised while they were ill. Perhaps if they hadn't have become ill, they would never have been saved? Katrina and I would almost certainly not have married had she been well enough to return to Bolivia. For that reason, I can even say I am *glad* she got M.E. She also now has contact with many families through her childminding and perhaps some of them will come to know God through meeting her and conversations she has with them. I recognise that Covid-19 has done a great deal of harm within not only our country but also the world. I am also convinced though that many people will come to know God because of this. Whether bereavement has made them think of God, or perhaps just having more time and the chance for a reassessment of life has caused them to 'look for' the 'something missing' in their life. We cannot know, but what we do know is that God works for good.

I guess ultimately what I'm trying to say is that we need to trust that God's plans are perfect. As I look back on my life, I see many things that I would have wanted to do differently at the time but hindsight has revealed that actually things worked out perfectly. God's plan or just a fluke? I know what I think, but I'll let you decide what you think. Often our perfect plan is not God's. We are looking at one level, He sees the big picture. As we become closer to God and know Him better, our plans start to align. Although we would still probably go about things in a different way, we learn to trust and accept that God knows best. It's an almost daily challenge for me to accept that God IS working out my life for what is actually the best, not just what I think it should be.

For I know the plans I have for you,"
declares the Lord,
"plans to prosper you
and not to harm you, plans to give
you hope and a future.

JEREMIAH 29:11

WHEN ANXIETY
WAS GREAT
WITHIN ME
YOUR CONSOLATION
BROUGHT ME
joy

PSALM 94:19

Time to let go?

By Alan Tyson

"No one sews a patch of unshrunk cloth on an old garment." **Matthew 9:16 & Mark 2:21**

We've all experienced a lot of change in our lives this year. At home, at work or school/college, when we go out or even because we're not able to go out. We're all adapting to the 'new normal' - humans are pretty good at this, although some people find it easier than others.

Many activities have moved online, others have changed venue and some are not happening at all. We've tweaked and altered and swapped around to enable life to carry on as much as possible.

By and large these measures have worked for the time being but are not necessarily desirable, efficient or sustainable. There comes a time when we must let go of the old and start afresh.

This is exactly what Jesus meant when he told the people that you can't keep patching an old garment or use old skins for new wine. In some cases this sort of thing can do more harm than good – the garment may tear even more or the wine and skins will be ruined. His coming, his teaching and ultimately his sacrifice were a new beginning. Everything that followed should take a new shape, build on a new foundation and be seen in the new light of his teaching.

I haven't got the answers to the problems that the COVID-19 crisis has caused but I want to encourage you to be open to new ideas and ways of doing things. They might take time to become established but once they are then do not be afraid to wave the chequered flag on the routines of the past. Similarly Jesus taught that the people of his time should completely replace the old human way of life with the new godly way of life – and letting go can be very therapeutic.

"No one sews a patch of unshrunk cloth on an old garment"

MATTHEW 9:16 // MARK 2:21

F(ear)fully and wonderfully made

By John Maple

I praise you because I am fearfully and wonderfully made; your works are wonderful, I know that full well. **Psalm 139:14**

I was sitting in the waiting room of Specsavers Hearing Centre, looking at the walls, when I saw some familiar looking pictures of the human ear. Well, I say familiar, but it was 60 years ago when I studied the human ear in Biology. Just to remind you, sound waves are gathered in the outer ear and travel down the ear canal to the eardrum. This causes the eardrum to vibrate and the vibrations are passed on and amplified by three tiny bones in the middle ear – the malleus, incus and stapes better known as the hammer, anvil and stirrup. (This is a bit of useful information for quiz nights because the stirrup is the smallest bone in the body – about 3.3mm long).

The motion of these bones causes the fluid in the inner ear or cochlea to swish back and forward. (The cochlea looks like a snail shell and cochlea is Greek for snail). The movement of fluid in the cochlea causes small hairs (stereocilia) to take up the swishing vibrations and convert them into electrical pulses which travel along nerves and are interpreted by the brain. Of course, this is just a simple outline, there are many other parts to the ear with complicated names. The ears also have other uses such as balance. They tell us how to stand up straight and whether we are twirling around or upside down. Personally, I prefer to remain upright and not be turned around like a merry-go-round.

While I was having my hearing tested, I said to the consultant, "The ear is a miracle isn't it" and she agreed, but I missed the follow up question, "Do you think God designed the ear or did it evolve by chance?" Perhaps I will remember to ask this next time.

When you think about the hearing process it is very much like a microphone. Sound vibrations are collected on a drum and converted to an electrical signal. It is just that the ear is a lot more complicated. We know that the microphone was invented by humans and has developed in many stages through people's clever designs. We would never say that it all happened by chance collisions of the necessary materials.

Sadly today, evolution theory is taught in schools as an explanation for why everything on the earth is as it is. Yet scientists have not been able discover how the very building blocks of life could have come together without an intelligent designer. Perhaps we will come back to this another time, but for the present, did our hearing evolve by accidental processes or was it designed? I think we have the answer in the following hymn.

O LORD my God! When I in awesome wonder
Consider all the works Thy hand hath made;
I see the stars, I hear the mighty thunder,

Then sings my soul, my Saviour God, to Thee,
How great Thou art! How great Thou art!
Then sings my soul, my Saviour God, to Thee,
How great Thou art! How great Thou art!

I praise you because I am fearfully and wonderfully made; your works are wonderful, I know that full well.

PSALM 139:14

Cheering you on

By Karon Jennings

The God of all comfort, who comforts us in all our troubles.
2 Corinthians 1:3-4

Dear sisters and brothers in Christ, I write this to encourage you all, for it is so long since I saw you all. Despite the opportunity of being able to connect via Zoom after the service, some six months down the line I have still not been brave enough to take 'the front row seat'. I'm not confident enough to do that. And I do not claim to be a writer, or preacher, or with any such gifts, but I wanted to be an *encourager*, for I have been encouraged by everything you all have done during this time of being a 'scattered church'. I don't want to leave anyone out, for there are so many of you who have continued through this time to lead us. So, when Andrew asked if I would think of doing a 'Thought for the day' my initial thought was my usual response, 'no', but then this verse spoke to me the very next day:

1 Corinthians 14:26 *When you come together, everyone has a hymn, or a word of instruction, a revelation, a tongue or an interpretation. All of these must be done for the strengthening of the church.*

I've read in some translations they use the word 'contributor'.

I wanted to share with you how I felt I should make something for someone. And I felt it had been placed on my heart to do this for someone. I'm not great at technology and I didn't think at the beginning of this virus we would be converted to getting our shopping delivered, but it made things very much simpler at the beginning of lockdown. And we've continued rather than go into the shops still. So, I hadn't done this recipe for a while, but felt sure I could remember what was required. I made sure I'd ordered what I needed on my delivery, and had brought something else from the market square on Saturday.

Arriving home, I decided that maybe I should just double check the recipe out, hopefully I'd remembered everything. Yes, I appeared to have everything, and then it jumped off the page: 'leeks'. And yes, I've heard all the stories about plastic bags leaking and deliveries not reliably being packed! But imagine my disappointment when I discovered I required one other item: a leek! Just one! And I hadn't ordered it on my Tesco shop.

So when my Tesco delivery arrived in the afternoon you can imagine my *absolute* amazement when I came across **leeks!** I double-checked the invoice, there were *none* listed. I hadn't ordered them. How did that happen? The Holy Spirit knew what I needed and knew I'd forgotten this one item, and made sure it arrived for me that very day.

2 Chronicles 20:15,17 *'Do not be afraid or discouraged because of this vast army. For the battle is not yours, but God's. ... 'You will not have to face this battle. Take up your positions; stand firm and see the deliverance the Lord will give you. .... Go out to face them tomorrow, and the Lord will be with you.'*

It might seem that we've all been in a battle at the moment with this Covid19, and feel like the battle is continuing. And maybe during this time you will all have been dealing with different battles within your four walls. *I* can easily be discouraged and, in my head, can talk myself out of doing *anything*, of my lack of courage and self-belief. But God has never given up on me, he's always there, patient and kind. He knows just what *I* need and he knows what *you* need as well. *I* think I'm on my own, and that it's *my* battle. But he tells me 'to take up my position; stand firm and see the deliverance the Lord will give you'. I hear myself saying, 'ask someone else', 'you can't mean me?', but every time I've 'trusted him' he never has let me down.

2 Corinthians 1:3-4 *The God of all comfort, who comforts us in all our troubles.*

The word 'comfort' means to encourage, cheer and come alongside.

When I hear myself saying 'yes', the mountain I think I cannot jump from ends up *not* being that *huge* leap but being small little steps and much easier than I'd expected. Many of you will know that we raised two of our grandchildren without the help of their parents, and finding *me* running a support group was definitely *not* on my agenda... for when we experience these things we become wiser. Hardship 'produces in you patient endurance' (2 Corinthians 1:6). Difficulties lead to patience, endurance, steadfastness and perseverance. We can come alongside others. And God says to us many times in the Bible *not* to be afraid or to fear or to be concerned. So even in this time, and with *whatever* you are experiencing, *our* God is with you. And I'm cheering you all on.

So, I want you *all* to know that I'm cheering you on. In the very early days of lockdown when we could exercise and we'd meet some church members whilst on our walk, I wanted to give a 'whoop' 'whoop'. It was *so* good to see you. I know I'm part of the 'body of Christ' and I will be standing with all my brothers and sisters in glory one day.

My story, God's salvation

By Eddie Boghossian

If you confess with your mouth, Jesus is Lord and believe in your heart that God raised him from the dead, you will be saved. **Romans 10:9-10**

For those who don't know me, I was born in Iran of an Armenian family. Being Armenian in a Muslim country wasn't always easy but was tolerable. Although Armenians are 'Christians' we used to go to church but only for Christmas and Easter, the rest of the year attending church only for learning to read and write Armenian.

In Iran dad had a good job, was second in charge of the telecoms for the Iranian oil company, but in the early 70's he realised that things were beginning to change in the country. He was right, as in 1979 the Iranian revolution took place; the Shah was overthrown and the country became an Islamic state.

Dad applied for early retirement, sold everything, bought GB pounds on the black market, filled a suitcase with the money and in 1972 we came to UK. He took the suitcase to the bank and deposited the money. It was enough to purchase a house, a car and furnish the house and put 3 of us in private schools.

Two years later, one Sunday evening mum went out for a walk and after a while she came back with an elderly couple who turned out to be an elder and his wife from a brethren church. Apparently mum was passing the church, she had heard the singing and had gone in.

On 29th July 1975, I gave my life to Jesus and **Romans 10:9-10** was one of the texts that led me to know Jesus. But then the question was, why do we need to know Jesus? **John 3:16** provided the answer: "For God so loved the world that he gave his one and only son that whosoever believe in him shall not perish but have eternal life."

In November 1975 I was baptised along with my mum and dad.

Whilst we were in Iran although we considered ourselves Christian, we had no idea about God, who Christ Jesus was, we had never seen a Bible nor heard a sermon. Therefore, we didn't realise at the time that God had been with us and had guided us with every step. It wasn't until we came to know Christ Jesus that the pieces came together and the whole picture became clear.

Praise be to God.

Wings

By Alison Wood

How precious is your steadfast love, O God!

The children of mankind take refuge in the shadow of your wings. **Psalm 36:7** (ESV)

Recently, I have been catching up with ABC school leavers, trainees, students and post-grads. Usually, at the start of the autumn term, we would share with you their situation to help you as you pray for them. As Andrew reminded us on Sunday, this year their experience is quite different to the one they had anticipated and looked forward to.

When our girls went to Uni, we reassured ourselves with the thought that we have given them wings so we should be glad when they fly. Then Bette Midler's song "I can fly higher than an eagle, for you are the wind beneath my wings," would get stuck in my head.

Wings and eagles are wonderful things. I know nothing about them, but there are people at ABC who can talk knowledgeably about updraft, drag, climb, power, swoop, soar, glide, thermals, lift etc. These words all came from one children's webpage about eagles. They are great words. I could suggest you use them in a piece of descriptive writing. But you don't need to. The Bible writers have already done it. The Bible is full of this imagery in praise of God. I've picked out Psalm 36 verse 7, but bearing in mind the new sermon series, I could have picked Exodus 19 verse 4:

> *You yourselves have seen what I did to the Egyptians, and how I bore you on eagles' wings and brought you to myself.*

Or Isaiah 40 verse 31:

> *Those who hope in the Lord will renew their strength. They will soar on wings like eagles; they will run and not grow weary; they will walk and not be faint.*

But I liked the ESV use of the phrase "The children of mankind," in Psalm 36:7. As well as knowing nothing about birds, my theological knowledge is also limited, so I am not going to define "children of mankind." My encouragement comes from the idea that whoever we are and whatever is going on in our lives (including students and their families), when our own wings aren't enough, we can take refuge in the shadow of His wings. Our God's steadfast love is there to shield us, or carry us through, or lift us up. How precious is that?

Do we always understand what we are reading?

By Kat Kouwenberg

Acts 8:26-39

Philip and the Ethiopian:

"Do you understand what you are reading?"

"How can I unless someone explains it to me?"

Part of my job is to make sure that the instructions for pregnancy and fertility tests are right before they are sent out to the printers. The products are sold across the globe and I am fluent in just one language. Trying to do this in a language where I don't even recognise the characters is an impossible job. I can look at the shapes of the text and make sure they match but I can't understand it. Thankfully I can use linguistic experts to help me.

When the Ethiopian official in the passage was reading the scriptures, he was having the same problem. He was looking at the words but couldn't understand what they meant to him. When we pick up our Bibles, how do we begin to understand them? Some of it is very plain, some parts we can understand and apply, other parts are harder or stranger. All these words were written so long ago in a culture very different from our own, should we even bother?

Thankfully we also have experts we can turn to, to help us: our church leadership, those we study with, Bible commentators and books all help. We also have fellow Christians, trying to do the same thing, to encourage and help us. And unlike my work task, we also have the ultimate expert to help us understand – the Holy Spirit. It is the Holy Spirit working through us that turns words on a page into something that lives and breathes in our lives. This all sounds super easy but too often I forget the basics, I need to invite the Holy Spirit to translate for me whenever I approach the Bible.

The Ethiopian found the truth of the scriptures and met with Jesus thanks to Philip, but Philip was not there by chance or on his own. From verse 26 to 39 we see that the Holy Spirit was working all the way through the encounter. Imagine what God could do through us if we allowed the Spirit to do the same every time we opened our Bibles.

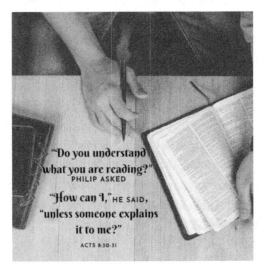

"Do you understand what you are reading?" PHILIP ASKED

"How can I," HE SAID, "unless someone explains it to me?"

ACTS 8:30-31

Facts and feelings: a sign of our times

by Dave Massey

Some media headlines that reflect many people's feelings – and sell newspapers:

- Second surge of Covid - "Fear we go again"
- Covid fear and frustration
- Lockdown desperation

How do I, as a Christian husband, father, and friend to others, respond to these times and try to articulate my thoughts to anybody who asks me?

I started by thinking about my namesake David and his thoughts in Psalms. Here was a man surrounded by so many enemies and who recognised his own frailties and fears. The first three verses of **Psalm 40** read:

I waited patiently for the Lord; he turned to me and heard my cry.

He lifted me out of the slimy pit, out of the mud and mire; he set my feet on a rock, and gave me a firm place to stand.

He put a new song in my mouth, a hymn of praise to our God.

Well, we are certainly having to *wait* and we have no idea

how long for.

How do we know he *hears our cries*?

Covid and lockdown, rumours and statistics, rules that contradict each other and then change, promises never quite kept, loneliness for many, and uncertainty for all. *Slimy pit and mud/mire* start to ring a bell.

Feet on a solid rock and a comfortable safe place to stand, that sounds good.

I would look forward to having *a NEW song in my mouth*, especially after sitting in church wearing a mask and being told not to sing.

I have to be honest, those were my immediate thoughts! But then, my cry out was to Jesus and he took me to **John 14 vs 25-27**:

> *"All this I have spoken while still with you. But the Counsellor, the Holy Spirit, whom the Father will send in my name, will teach you all things and will remind you of everything I have said to you. Peace I leave with you; my peace I give you. I do not give to you as the world gives. Do not let your hearts be troubled and do not be afraid".*

And **Philippians 4 vs 6-7**

> *Do not be anxious about anything, but in everything by prayer and petition, with thanksgiving, present your requests to God. And the peace of God, which transcends all understanding, will guard your hearts and your minds in Jesus Christ.*

These verses bring a phrase to my heart which has always helped me when I have felt loss or am not understanding why something is happening: "in sure and certain faith".

I know God sent his Son to earth (fact), sacrificed his Son for my salvation (fact), sent the Holy Spirit to keep me close to Christ (fact). I've prayed and been given peace (fact). Not the world's peace which is absence of conflict or positive thinking, or good feelings. God is in control and gives peace which is above our understanding, and protects our hearts and minds in Jesus Christ (fact).

I pray for all my family in Christ for this special peace and assurance during these uncertain times.

Peace I leave with you; my peace I give you. I do not give to you as the world gives. Do not let your hearts be troubled and do not be afraid.

JOHN 14:27

Don't worry, be happy

By Edd Moore

Go eat your bread with joy, and drink your wine with a merry heart, for God has already accepted your works.
Ecclesiastes 9:7

Life is a bit worrying and scary at the moment, so put your trust in God and you will find happiness, even when things go a little wrong.

I don't get many thoughts, so I thought I would share a couple of funny moments when things did not go quite right for me.

When I was younger, I was keen to find out about Jesus, so I went along to a Baptist Church Bible study group. We were sat in a circle reading through 1 Corinthians chapter 1, verses 20-31, one verse each, out loud. So I worked out which verse was mine, verse 24:

> "But to those called to salvation, both Jews and Gentiles."

So I read it over and over again to make certain I knew what to say, it was getting nearer and I was getting quite nervous.

My time came and I confidently started my verse:

> "But to those called to salvation, both Jews and the genitals."

I thought to myself that didn't sound right, but nobody

said anything, it was only afterwards that somebody mentioned the obvious error.

Oops!

Then there was the time a former Sunday school student invited me to his baptism. He texted me the time, date and address: 10:30am. 4th September. Baptist Church, West street, Dunstable.

So I turned up with plenty of time, parked the car and followed some other people into the church. I entered the church, with a big sign saying West Street Church. I was greeted by a lady who gave me a booklet and hymn book and I was shown to a seat. The service started and I was surprised by the lack of people I knew. Then a gentleman got up and read the notices, I thought: that's strange not to mention the baptism.

So I leant across and asked the person next to me, but he was not much use – he did not even know there was a baptism. Then he tapped me on my shoulder and said, "I think there is a baptism across the road at the Baptist church."

I was at the wrong church. So during the next song I sneaked out, crossed the road and went into the Baptist church, where I sat by an old friend. He asked where had I been, so I replied, "traffic was a nightmare." And I joined in with the singing.

Life does not always go as we think it should and sometimes we don't understand why. But I know I must learn to trust God more, remember that he is in control and he is faithful.

Be still

By Anna Irwin

The song 'Be Still' by Steffany Gretzinger is based on the Bible verse:

'Be still and know that I am God.' **Psalm 46 v. 10**

This is a verse that continually pops up in my life – whether in a sermon, a song or in Bible notes. I believe this is the way that God speaks to me, by bringing up the same verse over and over. I guess he's making a comment on my lack of listening skills!

I have always found it hard to **'be still'**. My brain takes every pause and fills it with trivial tasks or menial distractions. At Revels, the young adult small group, we were challenged to put aside just 20 minutes to be away from phones, laptops and any other distractions and just to wait on God.

To most, I imagine setting aside **20 minutes a day** to 'be still' with God seems like a lot. If it doesn't – good going and keep up the momentum. However, we often think as follows:

'It doesn't take 20 minutes to eat breakfast, so maybe I will do it at lunch. My lunch break is too short. Shall I do it

before or after dinner? I'm hungry, so afterwards. Oh, but now I'm too tired, I'll do it tomorrow.'

Sound familiar? This is certainly a thought process I often go through.

With a Masters in Mathematics, it only makes sense for me to follow suit and provide some stats about the time we spend with God. I always find it amazing how wording the same stat in different ways can provide a different perspective. **20 minutes is only 1.39% of our 24 hour day.** Or only 2.78% if you consider the day as 12 hours. Either way, dedicating roughly only 2% of our day to our Creator, Redeemer and Giver of life is not much at all.

Therefore my challenge to you is to give God his 2% and to 'be still' with him.

The big question

By Jack Moore

Jesus said to her, 'I am the resurrection and the life. The one who believes in me will live, even though they die; and whoever lives by believing in me will never die. Do you believe this?'

"Yes, Lord," she replied, "I believe that you are the Messiah, the Son of God, who is to come into the world." **John 11:25-27**

Many of you will know that I ask a lot of questions. For me faith has never been simple. Instead, I'll always find there is something new to learn or ponder. In the past this has often meant my faith can be on wobbly ground, as depending on the answer to a question I found my whole belief could come crumbling down.

In these verses, Jesus states that he is the resurrection and that whoever believes in him shall be saved. He then follows this up with one short and simple question. "Do you believe this?" Martha responds with a clear and confident declaration of her faith, assured of who Jesus is and his power, which is not something I would always have been able to have done.

I decided this was the one question for which I always needed to be able to give a confident answer, and I found this by focusing on the resurrection. This is the claim on which our faith stands, it is the centrepiece of the gospel that fulfils prophecy and is the assurance of our salvation. If the resurrection is true then regardless of our other doubts and worries, we can lean on this as the foundation of our faith.

So through prayer, reading the bible and a healthy dose of facts and evidence, I can now confidently answer that question with a resounding "yes, I believe".

By having a reasoned belief in the resurrection, I have gained a near unshakable evidenced based faith. I can confidently believe the resurrection really did happen. This took me off a rollercoaster of faith with highs and lows, and instead allowed me to continually deepen my relationship with God.

This confidence stands me on firm ground in evangelism, and can pull me through those periods of worry, doubt or hardship. It also means no matter what questions I ask, I can always be sure that Jesus died for me.

1 Peter 3:15 *But in your hearts revere Christ as Lord. Always be prepared to give an answer to everyone who asks you to give the reason for the hope that you have.*

We make plans...

by Sharon Cashman

Last week, fed up with online shopping, I went to Milton Keynes shopping centre. Ordinarily not an exciting trip to write about but these are not ordinary times. Equipped with my mask, bags, sanitiser, credit card and list I was ready!

Shops were quiet, awash with sanitiser stations and confusing entrance and exit routes but I found what I needed including ... a 2021 diary! Call me old fashioned but I like a week-to-a-page planner I can pencil in and carry around in my handbag to help organise my usually 'busy' life.

But in these 'strange times' do we need to plan? What should I write in my diary when most of it ends up being crossed out?

Proverbs 16:9 tells us *'The heart of man plans his way but the Lord establishes his steps.'*

Proverbs 19:12 reads *'Many are the plans in the mind of man, but it is the purpose of the Lord that will stand.'*

I have a (non-Bible) phrase I quote regularly: 'We make plans and God laughs at them.'

I'm sure over the past 8 months or so, you have had to postpone, cancel and adapt many plans, holidays and appointments which have probably caused you and many others great disappointment and upset. We have had a week on the Isle of Wight instead of an idyllic 2 week trip to Mauritius, but we valued that break enormously especially as we got to see family too (no more than 6 at a time) and the sea wasn't THAT cold!

Many of us have some control freak tendencies and become very frustrated, anxious and fed up being told what we can and can't do by Boris and his various advisors and politicians. Can we trust their changes and decisions?

What is not in question is our trust and hope in our constant God. He is there in the kindness of the neighbour leaving cake on your doorstep, in the phone call telling you of a birth or news of a pregnancy (note there is a 'quaranteenie' baby boom coming), in worshipping together again. God is in the detail of every situation and the community surrounding us.

Romans 15:13 *May the God of hope fill you with all the joy and peace in believing, so that by the power of the Holy Spirit you may abound in hope.*

And we hope we are not in a lockdown by the end of November when our 2nd grandchild is due to arrive.

Lives changed by God's grace

By Margaret Mozley

Love is patient, love is kind. It does not envy, it does not boast, it is not proud. It is not rude, it is not self-seeking, it is not easily angered, it keeps no record of wrongs. Love does not delight in evil but rejoices with the truth. It always protects, always trusts, always hopes, always perseveres.

1 Corinthians 13:4-7

When Andrew asked me to write something for Thought for the Day my immediate response was, "Oh no, not me! I can't do that. I'm a doer not a thinker!" During the long time it took me to gain any inspiration or confidence that my thoughts were worth reading, I did eventually come up with two things which seem linked in a way most appropriate for the times we are in.

The first was our son's recent wedding which, like many since March, was much smaller and more intimate than originally planned. Aaron, our son, had chosen hymns and readings which meant something to those present and he particularly wanted the Corinthians reading because he knew that we had it at our wedding 50 years ago next January. His curate took the reading as a subject for his address to the couple, talking about the power and purity of love and how these words were a reflection of God's unconditional love for us. They describe a lifestyle which we should aim to copy in our relationships with one another. He talked about trying to put your partner first each and every day, trying to uplift, encourage or comfort one another and in this way the marriage would be mutually fulfilling. BUT we are only human so we need God in our lives. His grace gives us the grace we need to cope with our human failings.

Then I thought about lockdown – how the world changed and how we changed with it. Suddenly families were thrown together "full-time" and with lack of personal space, the stress caused by the conflict of home-schooling versus working from home etc., it was easy to become irritable, angry and impatient with one another. Yet amidst all this it was frequently said that the world had become a kinder place; we met and talked to neighbours previously unknown; we had time for one another and people were saying they hoped it stayed that way when lockdown was over. It was inspiring to see how much good was done by ordinary folk raising money for charities, shopping for those shielding, fetching prescriptions for the elderly, baking bread, giving away garden produce, cooking meals or making phone calls to keep in touch with the isolated. The good thing about all this was that it wasn't only the receivers who were blessed, but the givers too. As with Aaron's marriage scenario, the process is mutually beneficial.

The most important thing for me in all this though is to remember, as Aaron's curate said, I need God. I'm so willing to help I often rush ahead and don't spend my energy wisely. I try to do things in my own strength. I need to pray more and listen for the answer so that, with God's direction, any help I give will be mutually beneficial too.

And now as I'm writing this there's talk of another lockdown at a time when the weather won't be so kind, when we are all rather tired of social distancing in a mask and long to be hugging again, when finances may well be tight and the future uncertain.

Can we do it again?

I am reminded of a traditional response, I think from a Christening/Baptism service:

"With God's help, we will."

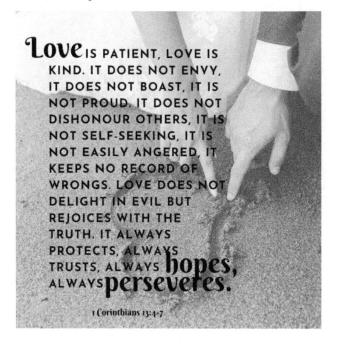

Love IS PATIENT, LOVE IS KIND. IT DOES NOT ENVY, IT DOES NOT BOAST, IT IS NOT PROUD. IT DOES NOT DISHONOUR OTHERS, IT IS NOT SELF-SEEKING, IT IS NOT EASILY ANGERED, IT KEEPS NO RECORD OF WRONGS. LOVE DOES NOT DELIGHT IN EVIL BUT REJOICES WITH THE TRUTH. IT ALWAYS PROTECTS, ALWAYS TRUSTS, ALWAYS **hopes,** ALWAYS **perseveres.**

1 Corinthians 13:4-7

Green pastures, still waters

By Karen Pigott

The Lord is my Shepherd, I shall not want. He makes me lie down in green pastures. He leads me beside still waters. He restores my soul. **Psalm 23, verses 1-3**

I have chosen these three verses as they have been a huge comfort to me over the many years I have been a Christian. As I reflect on these verses again and again, they never fail to revive, restore and refresh my very often weary soul.

I am so blessed to be living next to Great Ampthill Park where I walk daily on green pastures and by still waters. These vital visual aids never fail to restore my soul, bringing me into God's presence, often on my knees in prayer. It is a special place where I can just be ... me! It is a place of solace and has been a huge comfort to me, never more so than with the passing of my dear Dad last year, as well as the many trials that seem to come my way that very often overwhelm me beyond my own human understanding. God, my dearest Shepherd, never fails to meet with me and restore my soul.

The Lord is my Shepherd. ~ This reminds us that our Shepherd carries us on His shoulders with extreme, tender loving care. We can always rely and trust Him

139

with whatever is going on in our lives. He knows our needs before we do and therefore we come in total confidence knowing and trusting that He will guide our steps and will guard us from all evil.

I shall not want. ~ This reminds us that God provides our every need. What joy and blessed assurance we have in knowing that God who provided manna for the Israelites in the desert is still that same God today!

He makes me lie down in green pastures. He leads me beside still waters. ~ Just knowing God is in charge frees us from being encumbered in the vices and trappings this world has to offer. Satan may beguile us for a fleeting moment, boosting our egos. But we have a God we can lean on, and when we do, in total abandonment, His peace enfolds us in His unconditional love – no strings attached. How amazing is that.

He restores my soul. ~ God fills us with His radiant light so nothing from this world can penetrate it. How wonderful to know we have a God who can do that.

My LORD, My God
Oh comforter in the perishable storm
Light in the darkness of my hidden form
I cry out to you from the depths of my heart
in anguish, in hurt, in pain,
And there you are my Shepherd to pull me out of the rain
Draw me near to your comfort bliss
Lead me to your gentleness

And there, and only there my quaking form
Falls silent as your peace fills me anew
To restore my broken soul to awakened new.

I pray you all have a green pastures and still waters
where you can go and meet with God.

The Lord is my shepherd, I lack nothing.
He makes me lie down in green pastures,
he leads me beside quiet waters,
he restores my soul.

PSALM 23:1-3

Look up

By Karen Hornett

Look at the birds of the air; they do not sow or reap or store away in barns, and yet your heavenly Father feeds them. Are you not much more valuable than they? **Matthew 6:26**

I opted to go for a short walk around Coopers Hill during the first day of our second lockdown. It had been a trying morning and I needed a break to clear my head before refocusing on work.

As I returned from my walk and was just about home I looked up and marvelled at how blue the sky was. The whole time I was out I had been looking down at my feet, dodging the tree roots and trying to avoid rabbit holes. In doing that I had missed the beauty of the day and the sun bouncing off the incredible colours of the autumn leaves. I couldn't believe it. How did I do that?! As someone who adores blue skies I was shocked that I had paid so little attention to it and my surroundings. It made me realise that, particularly in these times, it is so easy to get bogged down in the negative and focus on the things that might trip us up and bring us down instead of the amazing things that are all around us if only we would lift our eyes to see it.

Whilst times may be difficult right now, we can rest assured in the knowledge that God is bigger than all of this and he loves you and cares for you. As Jesus said in the Sermon on the Mount, 'My Father knows what you need. Look at how much He cares for the birds and the flowers, how much more will He care for you?!'

Let's look up, lifting our eyes to Him and rest in that knowledge and assurance today.

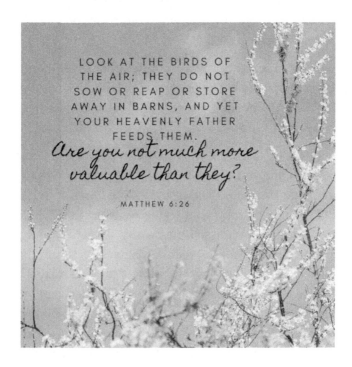

LOOK AT THE BIRDS OF THE AIR; THEY DO NOT SOW OR REAP OR STORE AWAY IN BARNS, AND YET YOUR HEAVENLY FATHER FEEDS THEM. *Are you not much more valuable than they?*

MATTHEW 6:26

Is your cup half full or half empty?

By Paula Moore

Trust in the Lord with all your heart and lean not on your own understanding, in all your ways acknowledge him, and he will make your paths straight. **Proverbs 3:5-6**

For many years, this Bible verse has been a real encouragement to me when life has thrown its challenges, and I've not been sure how to respond. I am not much of a writer, so I hope that by sharing with you, it will be able encourage you to stand strong in your faith, whatever your circumstances.

Some years ago, when Jack and Ellie were young, Edd and I were facing some uphill battles with his health, affecting his ability to work and eventually leading to him losing his job and career as an electrician. It was a difficult and dark time for us, while at times I felt desperate and alone. I have always tried to look at the positive, rather than the negative side of things but these circumstances overwhelmed us, leading me to question where was God in all of this, and what was his plan. One day a friend came to see me and asked me how my faith in these circumstances was? I remember quickly replying,

'Hanging on by a thread'. To my surprise she replied, 'Good, because you can build on a thread!' I was looking at my cup being half empty, but by looking at the situation in a different light I was able to have hope to build on that thread of faith that God helps us to hang in there. Having looked at our situation in a different light I have been able to persevere in my faith in God, knowing that I can trust him in all circumstances because he has a plan for our good. He taught me to be patient in my challenges and to trust in his promises. I am an organised person who likes to be in control of a situation, but I must learn trust in God's understanding, not my own as He knows what is best for us, whilst being faithful and true.

Edd was able to find work locally, for which we have always been thankful as it is a job that keeps him active whilst working with others around him, which in turn has had a positive impact on his health as he deals with the everyday challenges of living with Parkinson's disease. Many years later, as Covid-19 impacted the world, Edd had the security of his job during this difficult time for us all. We have both been blessed to have our work and our family together during these times. God has a plan for us, it might not be what we plan, but looking back I can see that, as we hold on to the Lord, having patience, trusting in him, building on our faith in our Father who cares for us.

I love listening to music and am often found in the kitchen preparing dinner with music playing. I recently came across a new song called *The goodness of God*. I have found the lyrics very powerful as God speaks to me through this song. [Look it up – it's by Bethel Music.]

We continue to face difficulties and challenges each day, but if I can be grateful and thankful for at least one thing at the start of each day, whilst reflecting on the goodness of God I can face the challenges of each day with my cup half full, trusting in God, knowing that He is with me and is faithful in His promises.

Your heavenly Father's care

By Rhoda Mortimer

> *"Look at the birds of the air; they do not sow or reap or store away in barns, and yet your heavenly Father feeds them. Are you not much more valuable than they?"* **Matthew 6:26**

I'd heard this verse many times, but the day it really stood out to me was in December 2008. I was sat in my kitchen, about to press 'send' on an email, cancelling my contract with a company who had provided 90% of my work for the previous 5 years (I was/am self-employed), questioning if I was doing the right thing. The company I had been working for had been taken over, and their values were in conflict with mine; I felt the right thing to do was leave, but the fear of cutting off my main source of income was real.

As I looked up from my laptop, just by our back door were two robins (my favourite bird). Nothing unusual there... except we'd never had them in our back garden before, let alone by the back door, and as I saw them God was saying to me, "Look at the birds, do I not feed them? I will feed you too. Don't worry." I pressed 'send'.

I felt like a weight had been lifted from my shoulders.

A robin for me is a constant reminder that God is there saying, "I've got this." It seems that whenever I'm anxious a robin appears prominently, right in my line of vision, or starts singing right beside me. It doesn't mean there'll be no hardship or pain, but it's reassurance that He's always there.

Look at the birds of the air;
they do not sow or reap or
store away in barns, and yet
your heavenly Father feeds them.
Are you not much more
valuable than they?
Matthew 6:26

God in the ordinary

By Judith Coen

But you, Bethlehem Ephrathah, though you are small among the clans of Judah, out of you will come for me one who will be ruler over Israel. **Micah 5:2**

Bethlehem was a significant city in the Old Testament, probably most notably for being the place where King David had been born and raised. However, by the time Jesus was born it had been reduced to the ranks of a small and rather insignificant village; nothing like Jerusalem with its palaces, citadels, theatres and monuments, all built by King Herod to increase his importance in the eyes of the Roman Empire. Surely Jerusalem would be the place for a new King to be born? The wise men certainly thought so.

But no, God chose the little town of Bethlehem, knowing that it would be weak and unimportant and 'small among the clans of Judah'. Out of this unexpected place came something so amazing and impactful, that we still celebrate it, in style, over 2000 years later; the birth of our Saviour, the Lord Jesus Christ. Like Mary and the shepherds, Bethlehem was ordinary and unremarkable.

I am the same and I expect you feel the same too; ordinary and unremarkable in many ways. What encourages me so much is that God used Bethlehem *because* of its ordinariness and not in spite of it. The joy and the light of the nativity shone brighter because of its impoverished surroundings. God's glory shines brighter in our lives because we are weak. I have never been more aware of God's power and glory than I have been over the last few difficult months. He has revealed more to me of His power and love at times when I have felt the most insecure and incapable. Sometimes I am disappointed by my own failings and inadequacies, but when I think of the Christmas story I realise that God works in me and through me *because* of them. I don't need to apologise for them, I just need to allow God to shine through them. He will change what He needs to change but He will also use my limitations to show His glory, just as He used the dark streets of Bethlehem.

My prayer is that we shall all know our value and worth in Jesus this Christmas and that we shall see the glory of the new born King in our lives now, just as they did in that little town.

Light in dark places

By Martin Sutch

Nevertheless, there will be no more gloom for those who were in distress. In the past he humbled the land of Zebulun and the land of Naphtali, but in the future he will honour Galilee of the nations, by the Way of the Sea, beyond the Jordan —

The people walking in darkness have seen a great light; on those living in the land of deep darkness a light has dawned. **Isaiah 9:1-2**

To those in darkness and gloom, a great light has dawned. That's such an encouraging idea to grab hold of, as it's what we long for, at the moment especially because so many of us can identify with being in a place of darkness and gloom. So easily I can paint a bleak picture of our society and mood under a cloud of Covid. The whole of society is suffering, unable to see friends and family, which is depriving people of the social contact that's needed, damaging health, both mental and physical, filling lives with more uncertainty than usual and increasing financial burdens, bringing even more issues and instability.

With my professional youth worker hat on, I am gearing up in anticipation of the response that will be required to this national crisis. Research looking at the long-term consequences of the pandemic highlight the disproportionate impact on young people. Just one element of that is school closures meant a quarter of pupils had no schooling or tutoring during the lockdown period and there's an inevitable cascade of knock-on effects that will cause.

One student says, "This is it, this is Uni. This is everything that I'd hoped for since year 7 and I'm sat by myself. As soon as you close your door to your flat it's so lonely and you spiral a little bit. It does lead to dark places."

Dark places. I'm finding it easy to write about the darkness and yet I feel that a message in Advent should be somewhat encouraging! But that is *exactly* the message of Advent. Advent starts from a place of darkness, this passage starts from a place of darkness. It's addressing people and places that have been scarred by oppression – fearful and without hope. People living in deep darkness, under fear of attack with an uncertain future. And then, the anticipation of light.

Darkness and light is a concept that is used right from the start of the Bible. In creation we have God casting light into the void, the division of light and dark. Then the rainbow, a symbol of God's promises and a hopeful future, a spectacle of light. And throughout this time of Advent we are lighting candles in anticipation of the breaking through of his light. It is so appealing to us right now in winter, in Covid, in struggles, in the dark when we can't see the way forward, to have a light. Light enables us to walk in dark places. People need light.

'Your word is a lamp for my feet, a light on my path.'
Psalm 119:105

Now, more than ever, introducing someone to Jesus, inviting them to journey with you, is providing hope in darkness. When those around us, those we work with, those who express to us that they are in the dark, our response is being hope-givers and light-casters, refocusing people on a light and a hope that they can walk by. Because we do have a light for our path. Covid has thrown us onto a path that isn't as direct as we were expecting, but I've found God rarely uses direct or simple routes for the business of transformation. We have inexplicable hope in life, through Jesus, in the darkest of places.

"I am the light of the world." John 9:5

The government will be on his shoulders

By Simon Herbert

For to us a child is born, to us a son us given, and the government will be on his shoulders.
Isaiah 9:6

One of the reasons that I like this time of year so much is that we get to hear and read many of the Old Testament prophecies looking forward to the birth of Jesus. This verse has struck me with extra meaning this year.

Looking back over the year of Lockdown I think I have been challenged most in the areas in which I have leadership responsibility. There is no management manual that speaks specifically to the period we have just been through. I have found myself still having to make decisions – at work, at ABC and at home – which impact people's lives and which influence the direction being taken by the organisations I am involved with. In "normal" times such decisions would be well-considered and taken after reviewing the facts and weighing up all the options. The last nine months has not afforded us this luxury and so decisions are taken and we pray and hope that we get most of them right. At times, I have felt the weight of this on my shoulders and have been grateful for the support of those I lead with to get through it all.

This verse from Isaiah is very comforting to me, to know that, when all is said and done, the government, the authority over and the leadership of all creation sits on the shoulders of the Saviour of the World. Hundreds of years before his birth, He was destined to assume His place of supreme authority. We can rest assured that He is not shaken by lockdown, His thinking is not confused, and He is not subject to changing science or social restrictions. He is not fickle, populist or corrupt.

We have become used to second-guessing our political leaders and being frustrated by the in-fighting and apparent self-interest. Thankfully, Jesus Christ is completely trustworthy and reliable. We can take comfort in His government and authority, not just over our lives but over creation, over history and over eternity.

FOR TO US A CHILD IS BORN, TO US A SON US GIVEN,

and the government will be on his shoulders.

ISAIAH 9:6

What do you want for Christmas?

By Ken Argent

When we were expecting the birth of our children, on each occasion we decided on a name and then changed the name when the baby arrived. When we looked at the new arrival the name we had selected just didn't seem to fit.

When God planned the first Christmas there was no such uncertainty. Several centuries before his Son entered our world as a baby, God described with conviction the names that would describe his Son's personality, character and mission. Isaiah the prophet boldly declared God's purpose with such conviction that he used the present tense!

> *For to us a child is born, to us a son is given,*
> *and the government will be on his shoulders.*
> *And he will be called Wonderful Counsellor, Mighty God,*
> *Everlasting Father, Prince of Peace.*
> **Isaiah 9.6**

When we changed our minds about naming our daughter it didn't matter much. We just wanted a name that sounded nice. In Bible times, however, names determined destiny and character and life's mission.

And so what did God give us that first Christmas, and what does he offer us again this Christmas?

Unto us a child is born, a Son is given, so that the decisions of life can be made with a wonderful counsellor.

The world needs wisdom and individual lives need wisdom. As I look back through the twists and turns of 75 years to the time I first entrusted my life to Jesus, he has indeed proved to be a 'wonderful counsellor' so long as I've let him lead the way.

Unto us a child is born, a Son is given, so that the demands of life can be faced with the power of mighty God.

At the front of the Church where I grew up there was a text which read: 'Jesus mighty to save and able to keep'. It was a great day when I discovered for myself the first part of that sentence and trusted Jesus as Saviour. Since that day, he has proved again and again to have the power not only to save me but he is able to keep me. If I am willing to trust Jesus I can have the confidence of the Apostle Paul who said, "I *can do all things through* him who *strengthens me*"(Philippians 4:13).

Unto us a child is born, a Son is given, so that the dimensions of life can be faced in relationship with an everlasting Father.

Where will life lead me? None of us knows what lies ahead. I used to run to my Dad when I needed help, or advice, or comfort ... but he died a long while back. God gave me at Christmas an Everlasting Father who has proved to be not just an Almighty God in heaven, as if He were remote from my personal feelings and needs, but a

Father who understands me and longs to have relationship with me.

Unto us a child is born, a Son is given, so that the disturbances of life need not frighten me because I am in the hands of the Prince of Peace.

When peace like a river attendeth my way
When sorrows like sea billows roll
Whatever my lot, Thou hast taught me to say
It is well, it is well with my soul.

That is what you and I are offered again this Christmas.

Last time I looked there were 138 **unwanted gifts** listed on eBay! Don't let the Wonderful Counsellor, Mighty God, Everlasting Father, and Prince of Peace be unwanted or ignored this Christmas.

Immanuel, God with us

By Marie Mead

"The virgin will be with child and will give birth to a son, and they will call him Immanuel" — *which means, "God with us."*
Matthew 1:23

How warm and comforting are Christmas films with their feel-good factor. You just know there will be a happy ending. However, films that tell the Nativity story are not like that. They clearly show the heartache and questioning of the characters, except for Mary who tries so hard to convince others whilst also facing the stigma of being pregnant before she was married. In one film it shows her nearly being stoned as an adulteress.

Also shown is the dismay of Joseph when he heard his beloved Mary's news and he knew it was not his child. As much as Mary tried to persuade him what had happened, he was not convinced, that is not until an angel came and told him. Not much good arguing then!

Being a Jew, he would have known the scripture above that was quoted to him by the angel. But surely that would not apply to his Mary? We know that he did 'the right thing' and cared for Mary and this very special child. What a tremendous responsibility... bringing up God's son.

Just think of the lessening of the impact if the events had

happened any other way. How could Jesus have truly been God's Son? He would have been just another prophet, but no: He was to be 'Immanuel'... God with us.

Our wonderful God did not want to be distant from those He had created but rather be up close and personal. How He longed and still longs for a close relationship with us. Imagine that, the Creator wants to come close to those He created and so He sent His son who laid aside His glory to become like us. He experienced what it was to be human and was 'God with us'.

Think of what Jesus faced in his life before He started his ministry. Those first 30 years were so special. Not only did He grow in wisdom and knowledge that was so important in his destined role but He also experienced so much. A refugee, a poor home, a hardworking existence, living in a family, working as a carpenter, having to deal with impatient customers, temptation, hunger, being tired, etc. etc. He was indeed 'God with us '. So, He knows all that we face and how we feel as He has been through it. So it is no good crying "You don't understand me or know what I am going through" because yes, He does.

How wonderful that He is always 'God with us' wherever we are in life, in the good times and in the bad, expressing his deep, deep love for us. Of course, His greatest love was shown at Calvary. Now He can be with us and us with Him forever.

So, during Advent, be sure to stop and remember that Jesus is our Immanuel – God with us – and be very thankful.

Be their star

By Pete Davies

"Where is the one who has been born king of the Jews? We saw his star in the east and have come to worship him." **Matthew 2:2**

Christmas is a wonderful time of year and means so many things to us all in our own way. Christmas for me as a child was exciting in lots of ways and I have so many fond memories of it with my family. We had sparkly and shiny decorations which were like tinsel origami that hung them from the ceiling and left sellotape marks when they came down. The tree was always too big which is how it should be! The milkman brought us our bottles of fizzy drinks: Cream Soda, Dandelion and Burdock, Cherryade and Limeade were such a treat! We all went to bed uncharacteristically early so we could get to sleep, which meant Santa would then come down our chimney (we didn't have one), deliver our presents and Christmas Day could start as early as possible, much to our parents delight.

In school we performed the nativity and we heard about Joseph and Mary travelling to Bethlehem on a donkey, that there was no room at the inn (*which at the time I always thought was a bit mean! Surely, they could have found a room for a pregnant woman*). We were told that baby Jesus was born in a stable and that three wise men travelled bringing gifts of gold, frankincense and myrrh and I don't think any of us knew what the last two were. How did we live without Google?

I wonder sometimes about the seed which is sown during Christmas in schools through the Nativity and how it grows. Every Christmas, primary schools all over the country reenact this incredible story. Parents with little or no obvious faith were telling their children about this epic journey, this string of events and coming together of people from far and wide that is the Christmas story and why we celebrate the birth of Jesus, yet many had little faith or any real commitment.

In Matthew 2:2 the wise men or Magi had travelled thousands of miles, searching for a king. These Magi were educated and of noble birth, rich and influential, and were most likely the counsellors of rulers and well-educated. Their journey would have taken months not hours and all they had to guide them was a star, which my study Bible says God who created the heavens could have formed to signal the arrival of his Son. They didn't have GPS, Satnav or Google maps. They were not forced but chose to make the journey, a journey which no doubt was very challenging, treacherous, and with certainty extremely tiring. All that they had learned throughout their lives drove them to do it. Search, follow a star, find the one who is born as a king – and remarkably they found him!

I take you back to that seed. To find your faith, each of us have travelled our own journey. For me I believe the seed was sown when I was young, through the Nativity, by my parents and the things they told me about Christ being born. I grew up, did my own thing for a while, made my mistakes, got in to trouble, had lots of great times, challenging times, treacherous events, made life-changing decisions and then I met Sheryl. After laughing when she told me she went to church, she cleverly got me to go with her one Sunday and after a time and lots and lots of questions, I found my faith. I found my King!

This year as we travel to see our families and friends, to spend valuable time with them over Christmas, some of them Christians, potentially many of them not, keep in mind that we ourselves didn't always know Jesus. We were once on a journey, our own expedition and – yes – as Christians we have found our King. Perhaps others are still searching and their journey is not over. Keep your faith, be their star and guide them on their travels.

Christmas will be different this year in so many ways due to Covid, but the story of Jesus and his birth and the events that preceded it will be the same forever, and those seeds will continue to be sown for generations to come by both believers and non-believers alike. We just have to help them grow!

BUT THE ANGEL SAID TO HER,
"do not be afraid,
MARY, YOU HAVE FOUND
FAVOUR WITH GOD.
you will be with child
AND GIVE BIRTH TO
A SON, AND YOU ARE TO GIVE
HIM THE NAME JESUS. HE WILL
BE GREAT AND WILL BE
CALLED THE SON OF THE MOST
HIGH. THE LORD GOD WILL
GIVE HIM THE THRONE OF HIS
FATHER DAVID, AND HE WILL
REIGN OVER THE HOUSE OF
JACOB FOREVER; HIS KINGDOM
WILL NEVER END."

Luke 1:30-33

The Son of the Most High

By Andrew Goldsmith

But the angel said to her, "Do not be afraid, Mary, you have found favour with God. You will be with child and give birth to a son, and you are to give him the name Jesus. He will be great and will be called the Son of the Most High. The Lord God will give him the throne of his father David, and he will reign over the house of Jacob forever; his kingdom will never end." **Luke 1:30-33**

We can become immune to the shocking announcement of the angel, that God was coming in person, and as a child.

The Christmas story centres on the birth of Jesus, the living God coming to us:

A 'child ... a son ... Jesus ... the Son of the Most High.'

Mary had more reason to be shocked as this was a very personal message for her. The scope of this child's impact and reign is one thing but, more immediately, Mary was to become a mother! So this child was her son too. There would be the bond of intimacy, love and joy between them, despite the unfathomable surprise at the angel's words. There is here also that powerful reassurance of God which has a familiar ring: "Do not be afraid." This still applies to us: following God does not cancel out our fears or mean we are always peaceful, it does mean we have the means to set fears aside, to conquer our doubts or anxiety, to find strength in God's presence with us.

This is Mary's firstborn on the way but he is also the Son of the Most High. Not something you'd see on other birth certificates. The living God, in all His fullness, is wrapped in the tiny frame of an infant boy (Col. 1:19). He's God the Son, in whom we get to see and hear the family likeness of God the Father. The Most High was arriving amongst us (the Very Low?).

As we approach Christmas, Advent is a season traditionally marked by acknowledging not the 'first coming' – the incarnation – but the 'second coming', that Jesus will return. We are in the waiting time, where darkness continues before light bursts in, the silence before the thunder of judgment, the steady growth of the kingdom before the King returns. The one to be born will be a fragile baby in a manger, but the angel tells us that he is great in power and majesty, one great enough to bear all our hopes and carry history to its conclusion, and his kingdom will never end. Advent darkness or covid darkness, deep as they may be, are not the last word.

So let us continue to bow our hearts and lives before him, let his kingdom shape our plans and desires, let his peace override our fears. For he is the Son of the Most High, who came to us, to rescue and to rule, to save and to lead, and he will return.

Rescued for a purpose!

By Shaggy Abdon Shortley

... to rescue us from the hand of our enemies, and to enable us to serve him without fear in holiness and righteousness before him all our days. **Luke 1:74-75**

I love visiting charity shops. I love browsing through stuff that other people have discarded – deemed "not needed" or "unwanted" – and imagining how I could put the item to use.

I once came home with what seemed to be useless pieces of wood and I made myself a couple of racks to hang my ukuleles on the wall. I was mighty pleased with the fact that I gave discarded wood a second life!

Sadly, there is a <u>limit</u> to how much I can 'rescue.' We have limited space in our house and there are limits on the time and skill I have to re-create stuff.

But – thank goodness – God's love, grace and mercy are <u>*limitless*</u> when it comes to rescuing us and re-creating us! He looks upon our brokenness, our sin and all that is wrong with us and, instead of discarding us, He sends His son, Jesus, who takes us – *rescues us* from sin and death – AND *enables us to serve him without fear in holiness and righteousness before him all our days* (Luke 1:74).

Like the bits of wood I salvaged to make something new, we are salvaged by God: given new life and given a new purpose. We are a new creation!

At Christmas, we celebrate the coming of The Rescuer of all rescuers: Jesus. As the carol *Hark! The Herald Angels Sing* goes, **Jesus** was

> *Born that man no more may die,*
> *Born to raise the sons of earth,*
> *Born to give them **second birth**.*

If you have put your faith and trust in Jesus, you not discarded, not broken, not rejected. You are rescued, dearly loved, forgiven and repurposed. This Christmas, let's celebrate His birth *AS WELL AS* our second birth!

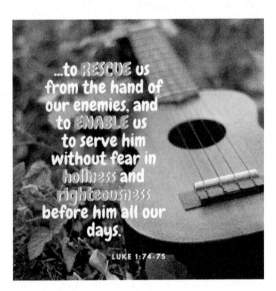

Wash and Worship no. 23

[Each week of lockdown Marie produced a 'Wash and Worship', which were so appreciated. This is just one example of this inspired art form!]

By Marie Mead

Dear all,

I am so pleased to announce that we now have a pond in our garden. After years of waiting we finally have one. It has stones at the bottom, ramps for the wildlife to get out and plants.

Now if in your mind's eye you have one of those superb ponds that so many have, you would be mistaken. Ours is 30cm by 30cm and is an old washing up bowl!

However, it is bringing us all such joy. What antics we see as the birds come and have a drink or a bath. What fun it is to see them queuing up to have their turn to use the facilities.

Queuing has become a natural part of life these days even to where you have to wait for your turn. The other day we are directed to a particular checkout. 'Go to till number 26' and when we got there, 'Stand behind that line' came the sharp call as we moved forward to unload our trolley.

I am just so thankful that when we want to talk to our Heavenly Father that there is no queue, no directive as to where we have to be, stand or what to wear. No allocated time slot, no one to tell us to go away as He is too busy to listen to us. Just come as we are, whenever and however... but of course with reverence and respect ... as we are coming into the presence of the Creator of the universe, the holy and powerful God who incredibly wants us to call Him 'Abba'. No high-sounding words or prepared phrases are needed for Jesus is there as well to intercede for us and the Holy Spirit translates our frequent mumbled, jumbled and incoherent words. How wonderful and reassuring is that!

I am reminded of this hymn which you may like to use as you wash and worship this week.

> *Before the throne of God above*
> *I have a strong and perfect plea*
> *A great High Priest whose name is love*
> *Who ever lives and pleads for me*
> *My name is graven on His hands*
> *My name is written on His heart*
> *I know that while in heav'n He stands*
> *No tongue can bid me thence depart*
> *No tongue can bid me thence depart.*

CONTRIBUTORS IN ORDER OF APPEARANCE:

Andrew Goldsmith, Shaggy Abdon Shortley, Diane Maple, Naomi Sherwood, David Mead, Marjorie Austin, Frank Sherburn, Mel Herbert, John Feil, Judith Coen, Pete Davies, Ruth Dant, Jo Reynolds, Martha Spencer, Tracey Feil, Rob Baker, Lauren Herbert, Patricia Royston, Gary Wood, Jean Eames, Steph Phillips, John and Cherry Parkinson, Carolyn Chappell, Lesley Taaffe, Ken Argent, Ruth Baker, Geoff Richardson, George Banks, Bernard Coen, Maryla Carter, Alex Vickers, Andy Harris, Claudia Tyson, Catherine Sleight, Michael Mead, Tim Darby, Jane Spencer, Ian Horsler, Gill Rowe, Gez Downing, Simon Miller-Cranko, Cheryl Spicer, Jim Widdicks, Alan Tyson, John Maple, Karon Jennings, Eddie Boghossian, Alison Wood, Kat Kouwenberg, Dave Massey, Edd Moore, Anna Irwin, Jack Moore, Sharon Cashman, Margaret Mozley, Karen Pigott, Karen Hornett, Paula Moore, Rhoda Mortimer.

Advent series: Judith Coen, Martin Sutch, Simon Herbert, Ken Argent, Marie Mead, Pete Davies, Andrew Goldsmith, Shaggy Abdon Shortley. *Wash and Worship*: Marie Mead.

Printed in Great Britain
by Amazon

34601227R00106